FOREWORD

During my 37 seasons with the Buffalo Bills, I wore many hats. In the early years I was not only the head trainer; I was also part equipment man, groundskeeper, janitor, carpenter, college scout and confessor. I never dreamed that someday my journey would lead me to don the hat of author, but here I am.

Endless thanks go out to Mr. Ralph C. Wilson, Jr., for allowing me the opportunity to begin and end my career in the same place without interruption, which is practically unheard of in the NFL, and for being the guiding force in bringing this book to fruition. During my time with the Bills, Mr. Wilson was much more than just my employer. He was and is a friend.

Many thanks are also given to Mr. Denny Lynch, who was instrumental in the creation of this book. His efforts are much appreciated. Much gratitude is owed to Mr. Milt Northrop who has organized and made sense out of so many years of memories. Without his help this book would not exist.

Over the years, I was privileged to meet so many great players, great coaches, and great people. Many lasting friendships were formed as I rode the roller coaster that included winning two AFL championships and four consecutive trips to the Super Bowl.

I am sure that on occasion, I have been referred to as a character. Well, to borrow an old phrase, it takes one to know one, and I have known many. From Danny Abramowitz to Connie Zelencik, and everyone in between. My memories seem infinite. I hope that sharing them with you, the fans, will enhance the memories that you hold while entertaining you with a few stories you had not yet heard.

More times than I can count, I have been told, "tell the one about..." Well, here goes...

This is me with one of my favorite young people, my adopted grandson, Shawn.

DEDICATION

My eight-year old grandson, Shawn, is a handsome boy with big, beautiful eyes and a wonderful smile. My daughter and her family adopted him when he was two, after caring for him as a foster child for many months. Shawn was born a normal, healthy baby, but had his life changed irrevocably when he was less than one month old. He was shaken and battered, and now suffers from Shaken Baby Syndrome. Shawn is unable to walk or talk, and he is significantly developmentally disabled. Although he is now happy and well loved, Shawn will live with the handicaps resulting from the injuries of his infancy forever.

Shaken Baby Syndrome is a severe form of head injury that occurs when an infant is shaken forcibly enough to cause the infant's brain to rebound against his or her skull. The condition is usually the result of non-accidental trauma or child abuse. Symptoms may include changes in behavior, irritability, lethargy, loss of consciousness, pale or bluish skin, vomiting, and convulsions. Generally, the prognosis for children with Shaken Baby Syndrome is poor. Shaken Baby Syndrome accounts for the majority of severe head injuries in children under 1 year old and results in over 1400 infant deaths each year in the United States.

To aid in the prevention of this form of child abuse, a portion of the proceeds of this book will be donated to the Shaken Baby Syndrome Program at Children's Hospital of Buffalo. Dr. Mark Dias, a neurosurgeon formerly at Children's, started the Shaken Baby Syndrome Program in December, 1998. This program is the first of its kind in our country to educate both parents of a newborn infant, and it is making a difference.

Thank you.

Ralph C. Wilson, Jr. and Abe worked together in pro football through five decades.

CHAPTER ONE

Meat burns and other
East Aurora mysteries

The kid was a linebacker from some college – it might have been Xavier — in Ohio. Maybe he was tough enough on the field, but not in the training room. This rookie was scared to death of needles and I saw the fear in his eyes when Dr. Sullivan came near him with the syringe.

He freaked out, jumped off the training room table and ran toward the door. He forgot one thing — the low bridge leading from the makeshift training room down to the main gymnasium floor at East Aurora High School.

Wham. He smacked his head into the crossbeam over the door and knocked himself out cold. I jumped up and began trying to revive him but Doc said, "Wait. Hold him down. I'll give him the shot while he's out."

And he did.

When the kid came to he said: "Geez, Doc. My ankle feels great, but my head sure hurts like hell."

That scared rookie was one of more than 100 players trying to make the grade with the first Buffalo Bills team in the summer of 1960. That should have been a tip-off right there that I was in for a wacky, crazy ride in my career as the head trainer of a professional football team.

I retired in 1997, but 41 years after that first training camp with the Bills, I'm still left with a million memories, hundreds of friends, a ton of unforgettable experiences and stories I've told and retold over the years about some great characters and thrilling moments.

Buster Ramsey, right, and Harvey Johnson.

My path to the Buffalo Bills actually began at the University of Detroit, where I was the head athletic trainer. On Sundays, I picked up some extra money as a game day helper to the trainer of the Detroit Lions, back in the years when they were playing at old Tigers Stadium. That's how I first met Buster Ramsey, who was the Lions' offensive line coach.

Nineteen-sixty was the year the American Football League started and Ralph Wilson, who lived in Detroit, obtained the rights to put a team in Buffalo. Mr. Wilson named Buster the Bills' first head coach and Buster asked me to come along with him as the trainer. I left the U of D with some regret. It was a good job, but they never gave you any raises. Working at a Jesuit school you got paid off mostly in titles. You know the old line: Jesuits take a vow of poverty. They take the vow; you get the poverty. I started there as athletic trainer, by the time I left I was director of sports medicine –- at about the same salary.

My family back home in Erie, Pa., thought I was nuts to leave the security of a college job to go work for the job with the new league. They all said the AFL would fold, but I figured, even if it did, it would be nice to have on your resume that you were a pro trainer. So, I took a shot. Besides, it brought me closer to home. Buffalo was only 90 miles or so from Erie, which I loved. All my aunts and uncles were there. I came from a big family. There were 10 kids on my father's side and 13 on my mother's.

Mr. Wilson has been a Lions fan since his dad began taking him to games in the 1930s. Because of that and because Buster came from the Lions, the Bills were a duplicate of the old Lions –- starting with the Honolulu Blue and silver uniforms and everything else.

We might have looked like a carbon copy of the Lions, but we didn't play like them. Of course, when Buster and I got to Buffalo, we were starting from scratch. We had no uniforms, no equipment, no players, nothing. Ed Dingman was hired as the first equipment manager and between him and me we had to order all the equipment — the shoulder pads, the helmets, etc., and we began collecting all the things you need to put a team on the field.

The first training camp was in East Aurora, N.Y., which is about 15 miles south of Buffalo. The team stayed at the old Roycroft Inn. The East Aurora High gymnasium served as our dressing room. All we did was put a nail on the wall for each player to hang his stuff, and there was just one stool for each player.

A little building connected to the gym served as the training room. It was very small, maybe 8 feet by 10 feet and cramped. That's where our young linebacker had the collision with the doorway trying to get away from Dr. Sullivan's syringe.

I remember that Ed Dingman and I stayed up until 4 a.m. the night before the first practice because we had forgotten to put the face bars and masks on the new helmets. We had to do them all, more than 100.

I hired a local high school coach to help me as an assistant trainer. He didn't know a lot about training but he knew how to do ankle wraps. We had more than 110 guys in camp at the start and we had to start taping them at 6:30 in the morning so they would be on the field for the start of practice at 10. Then I would start taping them all over again at 12:30 to get them all on the field for the afternoon practice at 4. Some of the guys used to leave their tape on from morning to afternoon so they wouldn't have to wait in line again.

That was my routine every day. It was a grind. Training camp lasted about eight or nine weeks. We had four weeks of two-a-days before we played any games. Then we had four or five preseason games.

The players traveled from the gym to the Knox polo fields on a rented school bus for every practice. We supplied the driver, usually one of the players. A player who could drive a stick shift and steer the bus became valuable – to a point. We always suspected that Buster kept certain players only because they could serve as bus driver and be cannon fodder for the first team in practice.

The guys used to say that if you could drive the bus you had a little security. John Scott, a big defensive tackle from Ohio State, was one of them. Some of the players suspected that the reason Buster kept him around for so long was because he knew how to drive the bus. Scott lasted two seasons, so he must have been either a good bus driver or a decent enough player.

The fields at the Knox estate were really hard from the pounding of the polo ponies over the years, but there were so many fields available that if you didn't like one, you would just move to another. There was very minimal maintenance. Dingman and I used to line the field and put up the goalposts. We didn't have any grounds crews like we have now. We didn't have a lot of practice equipment either. Buster had a seven-man blocking sled built and we had a two-man sled and a tackling dummy, but that was all.

I remember Buster visiting a training camp about 10 years later and seeing all those machines, sleds, dummies and other gadgets. "Hey, Eddie," he said. "What the hell you got all the machines for. Just have the guys hit one another. You'll find out who can play or can't play."

Buster was old school. He was against all that stuff.

"Hey, Buster," I said. "What can I tell you? You've got to go with the times."

He'd go crazy now if he saw all the equipment they have now, the JUGS guns, the video and the army of support personnel in a pro training camp.

We figured it out once. There are 17 guys doing what three of us used to do.

Buster had only three assistant coaches. Harvey Johnson was the talent scout and defensive backs coach. Floyd "Breezy" Reid coached the running backs. Bob Dove coached the line. We had no offensive and defensive coordinators. Buster did everything.

Breezy came into the NFL as a running back with the Green Bay Packers. He used to joke that when he came out of Georgia he was 6-foot-3, 200 pounds and had a 15-inch neck. After playing three years with Green Bay he was 5-11, had a 19-inch neck and weighed 240.

Buster brought Dove with him from the Lions.

We had all different kinds of players in that first camp: guys who didn't make it in the NFL, guys who played a few years in the NFL and a lot of kids just out of college.

Not all of them took it as seriously as they should have. We had one receiver out of Georgia named Norman King. Norman liked the ladies and used to sneak out after curfew every night. He'd shinny down the drainpipe from the second or third floor at the Roycroft Inn and head for where the watering holes and the ladies were. Who knew? I was too busy and tired.

Buster didn't catch on to Norman for a while. In fact, he thought Norman was one of his most dedicated players. That's because Buster would come down for breakfast at 6:30 each morning, and Norman was already there, having his breakfast. Buster thought King was an early riser and up-and-at-'em guy. He didn't realize — until later — that Norman had just gotten in from a night on the town.

"Look at that guy, King," Buster would say. "A minister's kid. There's a good guy. He wants to play football."

There was a rookie running back from Syracuse named Ed Coffin. When he started off in camp he was lining up with the first or second team and was really doing well. Then he started running around with King every night. Soon, Coffin's play went backward and he kept dropping down the depth chart until he finally got cut. Nobody could figure it out.

One of the rookies was a defensive lineman from Ohio State named Birtho Arnold. He weighed well over 300 pounds. We had to weigh him on the big scale at the Griggs & Ball Feed Store because he was too heavy for our scales in the training room.

He was so fat; he had to roll out of bed onto the floor, and then push himself up.

His thighs were so huge, they rubbed together and chafed when he ran.

One day Birtho came to the training room looking for something to put on the sores on the inside of his thighs.

I said, "What's the problem? Jock itch?"   "No," he said. "Meat burns."

CHAPTER TWO

One of Pinky's Boys

Besides my wife, Pat, and my parents, probably the two people who had the most influence on my life were Pinky Newell, the great trainer at Purdue, and my uncle Eddie Abramoski, who was a high school coach at Erie Tech and later became assistant superintendent of schools in Erie, PA.

Uncle Eddie was an influential coach and an innovative guy. He was one of the first to come up with the idea of a three-point shot in basketball, although it wasn't adopted until many years later. He also believed that when a guy gets his fifth foul in basketball, you don't foul him out of the game. Instead, the team that was fouled would get two free throws and possession of the ball. The rule change would ensure that the best players would stay on the floor and would be an answer to some of the "homer" calls star players get on the road.

When I was in high school I wanted to be a coach, too, just like my uncle. Uncle Eddie looked after me. He made me take all the right courses so I could get into college. I had algebra, trigonometry and all the English. When the recruiters came around I was a good college candidate.

A lot of schools were interested in me as a football player. I was a center my first two years at Erie East High and I played tackle my senior year because they were short of tackles, and the kid behind me at center was a real good player, too. Playing tackle I made All-City and honorable mention All-State in Pennsylvania.

We had a pretty good team. We lost to Cathedral Prep in a close game that determined the city championship my senior year.

*Believe it or not, I was an athlete in my day. Here I'm
practicing my shot-putting whe I was at Erie East.*

After the season I had offers from a lot of colleges — Princeton, Wisconsin, Harvard, Purdue and North Carolina.

I never did visit North Carolina because there was a story going around that the coach there, Jim Tatum, wasn't always totally honest with recruits. Supposedly, he would hide his first-string players when recruits visited practice. He would put the third and fourth string players on the field while the regulars were practicing out of sight somewhere else.

"See," he would tell the recruits who came to watch the team practice. "There's not much talent here. You'll be able to play as soon as you come in."

I decided to go to Purdue because of the Erie Connection. Bernie Flowers, Joe Suminski, Jack Konkol, Frankie Angelotti, plus we had wrestlers Dick Paterniti and Jack Gifford — all from Erie — were playing there. And, Stu Holcomb was the coach and he was from Erie, too.

Princeton was my second choice. I was a good student. Uncle Eddie taught me the importance of that. I also could have gone to Harvard, but they didn't give football scholarships and we had no money in my family. I was going to get a good award from Harvard, but Purdue gave me a full scholarship and I felt more comfortable with those guys from Erie already there.

As college freshmen in the fall of 1952 we were eligible for the varsity, due to the Korean War going on.

My first roommate there was Walt Cudzik, who later played center for the Bills. I would get up early every morning and go to the football training table for breakfast. Walt usually slept in. It was my job to wake him only if they had eggs, sausage and bacon on the menu. Anything else, he didn't want to be disturbed.

In the room next door was Tom Bettis, who also coached and played in the NFL later. When I went to practice I always had to wake him up.

My college football career ended early. At the beginning of spring practice in 1953 I hurt my back blocking on a sweep. I had to go to Indianapolis for surgery during spring break. I was in the hospital alone for almost two weeks. My parents couldn't afford to come down from

Erie and, except for Pinky Newell, nobody came from school. Pinky visited me once and then he came back to pick me up when I was released from the hospital.

At first the doctors said I would be able to play again. But three weeks after I got back to school I had more pain. And they went in and operated again. After the second time they said, "no, you can't play anymore."

Two discs in my back were bulging. I have a scar 4-5 inches long on my back. I don't know exactly what they did— shave the disc or what; I've got a lot of arthritis there now. If the same injury happened in this day and age, I probably would be able to play, there's no doubt in mind.

It wasn't easy watching instead of playing, knowing I was as good as guys who were playing, but you play the hand you are dealt. I still wanted to coach, but then I thought to myself: Who's going to want a coach who has no experience as a player?

I had played one year of college football. It was going to be hard to get a good job even though my uncle had some influence in Erie. I didn't like my chances of going far in coaching: You're going to start teaching physical education in grade school or junior high.

Even though I couldn't play any more, I wanted to be around the team. So, in my sophomore year, I took a job as a student trainer to keep my scholarship and be around the boys. That's when Pinky Newell took me under his wing.

Pinky was one of the finest trainers in the country. He was one of the leaders in making it a true profession. Working in the training room, I learned to tape very fast and got pretty good at it. Pretty soon a lot of guys were coming in for me to tape them.

In the years I was in the Purdue training room, one of my roommates was Kenny Panfil, a tackle who later played in the NFL. He was one of the players the Los Angeles Rams traded to the Chicago Cardinals for running back Ollie Matson, in one of the biggest deals in NFL history. My other roommates were Joe Krupa, who later played for the Steelers, and Dick Skibinski, one of the famous brothers who played for Purdue.

Panfil was from the Gage Park area in Chicago, right behind the stockyards. I remember once staying at his house on a weekend visit. I didn't sleep very well. All night I could hear the trains bumping and all the other noise from the stockyards. And, it smelled bad.

Pinky was like a father to me, especially in my senior year after my dad, Alex, died. He died at age 62. My mom was 52 when she died.

My dad had spent a lot of time in the Navy in World War II. He served as a millwright on one of the ships that was captured from the Germans. Our navy refitted it, renamed it and used it against the Germans.

After the war, Dad came back to Erie and worked at the Detroit Steel Mill. At home he was a real handyman. He could fix anything. We bought a house and he put the roof on it. He put the aluminum siding on it. He plastered. He did electrical work. He did all the stuff.

Pinky gave me a lot of good advice as I looked ahead to a career as an athletic trainer. One thing he taught me — and it's something that stayed with me as long as I was a trainer –- was that you treat every guy on a team the same, from the No. 1 to No. 53, or whatever you have. If you start showing favoritism, guys will lose respect for you.

That meant you had to treat some guys you did not like the same way as those you did like. I have to admit there were a few guys on the Bills I taped for 12-13 years and really disliked or did not respect. They would come in and hug me and say what a great job I did for them. Really and truly, I disliked some of them big time.

Pinky practiced what he preached. He played no favorites. We had a pretty good running back at Purdue named Max Schmaling. One day, when I was just learning how to tape and still pretty new at everything, Max was late getting to the training room for taping before practice.

I had nobody in line at my table and Pinky had a long line waiting for him. Max headed for Pinky's table without hesitating.

Since Max only wore ankle wraps, not a full tape job, Pinky told him, "Jump on Eddie's table."

Max said, "I'm not going on that kid's table. He doesn't know how to do anything."

Pinky said, "My man, you're going on that kid's table or you're not getting taped."

When Schmaling refused, Pinky said, "Well, get out of the training room." And he threw him out.

The way Pinky backed me up made me feel good.

Many years later, when I was with the Bills, Jim Kelly was our star quarterback. He would come in before practice in a hurry and try to jump the line. I would tell him, "Hey, Kelly, get at the end. Wait your turn."

Jim would yell and complain but end up doing what I said. Deep down, I knew they had respect for me because the next day they were in line again.

When I finished at Purdue, I was supposed to go to physical therapy school at the University of Pennsylvania. Pinky wanted all his guys to be physical therapists in addition to being licensed athletic trainers. I was one of the few from Pinky's program who did not go to physical therapy school. Because my dad had died in my senior year I needed to help my mom and sister at home. I decided to take a job rather than go on to graduate school.

During my time at Purdue, Stu Holcomb had left and gone on to Northwestern. I was offered the assistant trainer's job at Northwestern and I had offers from Western Illinois and from West Point. The job at West Point paid $300 more, $4,300 for nine months, while Northwestern was going to give me $4,000 for 10 months. Also, West Point was closer to home in Erie, so I took the West Point job.

CHAPTER THREE

In the den of the Lions, Tigers and Titans

When I got to West Point I hated it with a passion. The military regimentation was not for me. After two months I told Pinky I wanted to leave.

"No, Eddie," he said. "Look, you signed a contract. Stick it out and use it as a learning experience. If you ever become a head trainer don't do those things that you didn't like."

There were a lot of little things about working at West Point that drove me crazy. Once we were playing some pickup basketball on our lunch break — me and some enlisted guys against some officers. The ball went out of bounds off a lieutenant, but he calls "my out."

"No. It went off you," I argued and turned to Pete, the corporal I was playing with, and said, "Tell him it was off him. You were guarding him."

Pete said, "No. It's his out."

Afterward in the locker room I said to Pete:

"You know damn well the ball went out off him."

"Yeah," he said, "but I work for him. I didn't want to piss him off."

I was the trainer for the hockey team and we were playing Royal Military College from Canada. Ordinarily only a few officers used to show up for the games, but a lot of them would come to this one so they could hob-knob with the Canadian Army officers.

When I pulled up to the parking lot next to the rink a couple of hours before the game to unload my equipment, like I usually did, they had a

Abe and Pat in Detroit.

guard posted. "Sir, you can't park here," he said. "This lot is reserved for officers tonight."

"But," I said, "I park here for every game so I can unload all my equipment. The nearest parking lot is a half-mile away."

"Sorry, sir," he said. "Those are my orders."

Stuff like that blew my mind. I'm sure they do it for a reason, but it just wasn't my cup of tea.

The great Earl "Red" Blaik was the football coach at Army when I was there. Since I was from Purdue, he would always ask me how his teams would fare playing in the Big Ten.

"Coach Blaik," I'd tell him. "Your tackles weigh 190 pounds. In the Big Ten the tackles are 230-240. You'd get killed."

That used to drive him crazy.

The old Army fullback Felix "Doc" Blanchard was helping coach the team when I was there. Because Doc was an Air Force fighter pilot, Army had one advantage over other schools. Rather than wait for game films from next week's opponent to be shipped in on Monday, Blanchard would take a jet fighter and go get the film a day ahead of time and get in his flight time in the bargain.

When the varsity football team was away for a road game, the head trainer would leave me in charge of the trainer's room. Once while I was in charge, somebody took two lemons from the refrigerator in the training room. When my boss came back on Sunday with the team, he had a fit over the missing lemons. I got so tired of hearing him complain, I went out and spent 10 cents, or whatever they cost, and replaced the missing lemons.

When I finished the year out at West Point, I got lucky. Millard Kelly, the trainer for the Detroit Lions who was a Purdue graduate, called me to work training camp for the Lions. While I was there in the summer the training job at the University of Detroit opened. I applied for that and I got it. At the time, I was the youngest head trainer at an NCAA Division I school. I'm sure Pinky Newell had a hand in my good fortune.

I really loved the University of Detroit. I had a terrific friend there in

Father Norbert Heutter. We did a lot of things together. He ran the bookstore for the college. He got the books for the athletes, got them tutoring. Father Heutter and I would do different things together -- go to ballgames, the movies. He'd hear confessions from the nuns and then we'd go out and have dinner somewhere.

That's how I did my pre-Cana before getting married. We did it one-on-one with Father Heutter.

The coaches at the U of D were terrific, too. Wally Fromhart was the head football coach. We also had John Ray, who was the head recruiter for football. Later, he coached with Ara Parseghian at Notre Dame and then was head coach at Kentucky. He coached with the Bills in the '70s, too. We had some good players at Detroit — John Dingens, Grady Alderman, Bruce Maher, Emerson Dromgold, Joe Pascuzzi, Tony Sterlitz and Joe Faoro were just a few.

Another good guy was Bob Calihan, the basketball coach. I really enjoyed basketball a lot. I was there when Dave DeBusschere started his career at the U of D. Another good player was Charley North.

While I was at the U of D, I still helped the Lions out as a game-day trainer and helped out in training camp at Cranbrook School.

I was at training camp with the Lions in the heyday of quarterback Bobby Layne and defensive tackle Alex Karras, two of pro football's greatest characters.

The Lions were notorious pranksters and had a lot of fun. Layne, of course, was famous for sneaking out after curfew and enjoying the nightlife. He was always looking for guys to keep him company. Some of the guys needed their rest and the last thing they wanted to do was stay out night-clubbing with Layne and risk missing bed check and a good night's sleep. When Bobby came looking, alot of the players would hide, often in the bathroom stalls. They would stand on the commode so Bobby would think nobody was in there.

A guy that Layne usually tried to corral was Harley Sewell, a guard, who was a fellow Texan. Layne used to make him go out all the time. They would pay his fine if he got caught breaking curfew. The same with Karras. They'd play poker and send Karras out for pizza and they would pay his fine out of the chips in the pot if Buddy Parker, the coach, caught him out after curfew.

Lions training camp where I first ran across Jack Kemp, who later was our quarterback with the Bills. Kemp tried out with the team and was on the taxi squad. The Lions players claimed the only reason Parker kept him around longer than usual was because Buddy's hometown was Kemp, Texas. He was superstitious about things like that.

I also picked up some extra money working for NBA teams when they came to Detroit to play the Pistons. Most of them didn't travel with a trainer in those days, so I would take care of them.

A few times Millard Kelly and I helped out with the Tigers, too. It was amazing to me that there were guys in baseball who wouldn't play a game because they had a headache or an upset stomach or because they were out late the night before and didn't feel good.

That was one thing about Layne: As much partying as he did, he was always ready to go the next day, no matter how he felt.

Another great thing about working in Detroit is that's where I met my wife, Pat. She was there on affiliation from St. Joseph's Hospital in Ann Arbor, working at the tuberculosis hospital in Detroit. One night, some of the guys at the U of D were going over to the hospital to meet these girls. They didn't have a car so they asked me to drive over with them. That's how I met Pat. She's been my bellwether all these years.

I loved my three years at the U of D, but I knew I would never become a wealthy person working there. When the Bills job came along, I figured it was a good opportunity. Next thing I knew, I was off to Buffalo.

The dynamic duo of the early sixties -- Cookie Gilcrest running behind Billy Shaw.

CHAPTER FOUR

"Mares Eat Oats . . ."

The Buffalo Bills were not an overnight sensation under Buster Ramsey. We were 5-8-1 the first year, in 1960, and 6-8 in 1961. We had good support, but the fans were getting impatient. So was Mr. Wilson, because Buster got fired after the second season.

Though we may not have been winning a lot, life with Buster was never dull.

Buster would always say he would want things done democratically. When it was time to cut players in training camp, he always wanted us — the coaching staff and me — on hand to help with the decision.

He would write the names of the players on a blackboard and we would go over them one by one. "Tell me your opinion," Buster would say. Sometimes the assistant coaches and I would all agree that a guy should be kept, but after we'd get through with the discussion, Buster would say, "He's gone," and erase the name from the board.

That was the end of democracy with Buster.

We had a seven-man blocking sled, but they didn't use it to work on blocking. They used that sled to get guys into shape. Buster had them push it the length of the field. Because the guys didn't come to camp in shape, they used the first four weeks of camp to get ready before we started playing the games. These days, everybody comes to camp in terrific shape.

We had the Ramsey Rolls as punishment for curfew-breakers. Buster would make the guilty players roll 100 yards and they would all get sick. He had no mercy. "When you taste hair, swallow," he would yell at them. "Because that's your asshole."

Elbert Dubenion (left) celebrates after the 1964 championship game with owner Ralph Wilson (center) and coach Lou Saban.

Buster was as hard-nosed as you could be.

Long before Woody Hayes got fired for slugging an opposing player in a bowl game, Buster did the same thing.

We were playing the New York Titans in 1961 and Al Dorow, the New York quarterback, scrambled out of the pocket toward the sideline. Our cornerback, Richie McCabe, who was quite feisty, hit Dorow long after he was out of bounds. Dorow got up and threw the football at McCabe. With that Buster turned Dorow around and punched him right in the chest.

After the game Buster knew he was in line for a league fine. "Eddie," he said, "I didn't hit him, did I?"

Yeah, Buster, you did," I said.

Buster would never talk about the incident and never admit how much he got fined.

Harry Wismer, the Titans' owner, made a big deal about the incident, probably to spark some interest in his team, which was losing money at the Polo Grounds. Eventually, Wismer sold the team to Sonny Werblin's group and the New York Jets were born.

In our first year, Buster called a reverse to Elbert Dubenion on the opening kickoff for three consecutive games. It went for a big gain the first time, but the next two times Duby got smeared.

Now we're getting ready for the fourth game and Duby was dreading another reverse on the first kickoff. He asked Buster what the strategy would be this time.

"Don't you think they'll be looking for the reverse, Buster?" Duby said.

"Hell, yes, I'm sure they'll be looking for the reverse," Buster said.

There was silence for a few moments, Finally, Duby asked him what return to run.

"Run the freaking reverse," Buster said, without breaking a smile.

Naturally, Duby got smeared again.

Buster was tough to take after a loss. When we'd lose a game on the road, all the guys would pretend they were sleeping on the flight back home because Buster would go down the aisle and berate each one individually.

Buster also kept players on the roster for odd reasons. I mentioned how he kept players around because they knew how to drive the team bus. We had a guard from Wisconsin, John Dittrich. Buster kept big John around because he played the spoons. He wasn't any good as a player but he was good entertainment for Buster.

After a win on the road, Buster used to like to make us sing on the trip back. Once he insisted I sing, too. I sang that old Bing Crosby song, "Mares Eat Oats and Does Eat Oats and Little Lambs Eat Ivy." The players gigged me about that for a long time. To this day, some of them still break out in "Mares Eat Oats..." when they see me.

Buster was a creature of habit. He'd make Dr. Sullivan bring $100 in fresh dollar bills on every road trip so they could play Liars' Poker on the plane. We flew prop planes then. It took six or seven hours to come home sometimes from the West Coast, usually with a refueling stop. So there was a lot of time to kill.

Once, we even shared a plane with our archrivals, the Boston Patriots. We both were going out West for games. The plane picked up the Patriots in Boston, then stopped in Buffalo to pick up the Bills. Then we were dropped off in Denver and the Pats continued on to Oakland for their game.

I often wondered what would have happened if the plane crashed and we lost 25 percent of the players in the American Football League, not to mention 25 percent of the trainers.

Over the years I spent with the Bills, we had only a few scares traveling by air.

In 1973, we were on our chartered flight to New Orleans and I looked out and saw some kind of fluid running off the wings. I was sitting with Dennis White, who had been a jet pilot before he joined our marketing department.

I pointed out what I saw to Dennis. "Oh my God," he said. "That's hydraulic fluid."

Seconds later, the pilot got on the intercom and said we were diverting to Pittsburgh because of our hydraulics problem. After a while, he announced we were going to Cleveland instead because they have a longer runway.

He took us out over Lake Erie so we could jettison most of our jet fuel and then we began our approach into the Cleveland airport. Without hydraulics we couldn't get the landing gear down. The co-pilot had to manually crank the wheels into place. We then flew over the airport so ground observers could confirm that the landing gear was locked into place. The pilot set the plane down perfectly and as we taxied down the runway we could see the fire trucks lined up just in case.

They towed us to the terminal and everybody – coaches, players, trainers, and team officials – made a mass exodus to the bar. Later in the day they brought in another charter plane and we were on our way to New Orleans.

Needless to say a shaken Bills team lost the next day to the Saints.

I didn't have a fulltime assistant until the Bills hired Bob Reese in 1972. Working alone most of the time got pretty hectic. I would be treating one guy and taping another at the same time. While I was taping I sometimes had to stop to put ice on a guy who was getting treatment or watch a guy do some rehab exercises.

Coaches always wanted the team on the field at a certain time so you had to have the players all taped up and ready to go. In those days I could tape two ankles in probably two-and-a-half minutes. You had to be fast and you had to know how to motivate a guy to do things to help himself. For example, if you had a guy come in and he was supposed to stretch, you didn't have time to watch him to see if he did it properly. I would show the guys how to do the stretching exercises and they would do them.

After the first two years, there was enough work to keep me busy the year 'round. I even did some scouting for them. They sent me to Utah, Wyoming, North Dakota, South Dakota, Idaho — hard-to-get-to places that the other scouts didn't want to go to. I recommended a few players. I remember going to Utah State when Tony Knap was the coach there. He had some prospects. I recommended one, Spain Musgrove, a defensive lineman who was a No. 1 pick of the Washington Redskins, and a guard, Jim LeMoine, whom we drafted.

I sat in on the scouting meetings. Harvey Johnson was our talent scout. Harvey wasn't the best organized scout there was – he would have notes scribbled on little pieces of paper in his pocket — but he had an eye for talent and connections in football that soon began to pay off for the Bills.

The seal of the former AFL.

CHAPTER FIVE

Marchitte: A real "G.G.!"

When Ed Dingman, our first equipment manager, got drafted and sent to Vietnam, Buster hired Tony Marchitte to take his place. Marchitte was a bartender at Ace's Steak Pit, a place in downtown Buffalo near the Bills' old offices on West Mohawk Street.

Buster and Tony got along well. One day, the coach asked Tony, "You want to become equipment manager?" Tony took the job and the rest is history. At first, I had to teach Tony everything but in a couple of years he could change a facemask or repair a chinstrap on a helmet quicker than I could.

Tony would say, "See, Polack, I'm twice as fast as you now, buddy."

I said, "Tony, you should be. You do it every day. Can you tape an ankle?"

"Give me a day or two. I'll be able to do it," he boasted. Tony was never caught without an answer. He became not only a close colleague but also one of my best friends. For the next 20 years or so, before he retired, we roomed together on road trips.

When Tony worked at Ace's I used to stop in for a sandwich at lunchtime. Tony would take my order and yell over to the guys on the grill, "One beef on weck. G.G."

One day I asked him, "Why do you say 'G.G.?'"

Tony explained that he and the chef had a little code. "G.G." meant good guy. If Tony said that, you got the best treatment — the tenderest slice of roast beef or maybe even a little extra. If he said "N.G." you might get a piece with a lot of fat and gristle.

Tony Marchitte in unifrom with Saban.

Tony had good rapport with the players, especially the black players. They really liked Tony because he didn't patronize them. He treated them rough, like he treated everybody else. If you asked Tony for something, a piece of equipment or an extra pair of sweat socks or a T-shirt when other players were around, you'd get the Marchitte Treatment. It would go something like this:

"Tony, can I have a new pair of socks?"

"You ain't getting any socks from me. What did you do with the other ones? You come in here bare-ass and now Wilson is clothing you. How many pair you got at home? Bring them in and you won't have to do this."

On the other hand, if you approached him quietly, in private, and asked for something, Tony would say:

"Come in the back. I'll give you a pair."

Tony had his own way of dealing with players who didn't pick up after themselves in the locker room, leaving dirty towels, socks and equipment laying around.

Leave a T-shirt and jock strap and socks on the floor in front of your locker, Tony would pour cold water on them and leave them. He wouldn't give you any fresh stuff, which meant the players had to practice or play in cold, damp, smelly jocks and socks.

Usually they got the message and learned to pick up after themselves.

In Tony's first year on the job, Chuck McMurtry, a defensive lineman, complained that his new helmet was too tight.

Marchitte thought it fit right and kept putting McMurtry off. Finally, Tony agreed to send the helmet back to the manufacturer to get it stretched, telling McMurtry it would be back in a couple of days. Instead, however, he just hid the helmet away in the back of a shelf in the equipment room.

McMurtry came in a few days later and tried on the helmet and was satisfied with how it fit.

"See, Tony," he said. "This is the way it was supposed to fit in the beginning."

There was a time when we were having a problem with stuff leaving the equipment room — shirts, socks, shorts and stuff. Management finally instituted a policy where everybody had to sign for every item of equipment they took.

One day Ralph Wilson, the owner, came in and asked for a couple of Bills golf shirts for his friends.

Tony gives him the shirts, then says, "Here, Mr. Wilson. Sign here."

Ralph took it with good nature.

"Tony," he said. "You're just doing your job, aren't you?"

Tony and I roomed together on road trips. We could have roomed singly but we doubled up all the time. He was really a good person.

I remember one trip to New York for a Monday night game. It's the morning rush hour and when I awoke, Tony was already up. He was sitting by the window looking down at the traffic gridlock in the street below.

"Hey, Polack, wake up," he said. "Look at those poor bastards going to work. Here's you and I in the best hotel in town because of some damn football game and getting ready to go down and have a big breakfast on Ralph."

Tony was so popular that when he retired old Bills players came from all over the country to honor him. O.J. Simpson made a special trip from Los Angeles to be there. One of the guys, Mike Stratton, took the time to write a poem about Tony, which he read that night.

> The disposition of a wounded buzzard,
>   The looks of one, too;
>
> The sarcasm of a mockingbird,
>   To which nothing is ever new;
>
> The gruff garble of a turkey's gobble,
>   Which he believes everyone is due;
>
> The caring kindness of a mother hen,
>   And the private softness of a pigeon's coo;
>
> Tony Marchitte, all these fowl things are you.

When Lou Saban was coach, we had a tradition to mark the closing of training camp.

Marchitte would dress up in a uniform and pads and come out late to practice. Lou would stop practice and "cut" him right then. Tony would act dejected and go back to the locker room and come back out with a keg of beer for the players to mark the end of practice.

Tony was always looking out for the little guy. Once, he and I were eating in a restaurant on the road and one of the assistant coaches was at a nearby table. When the coach left, he shorted the waitress on the tip.

"That cheap bastard," Tony said. He called the waitress over and gave her $5 out of his own pocket.

The trainers and the equipment guys are always the last ones to eat at the training table in camp. Once, when we were practicing at the Regency Hotel in Blasdell, spaghetti was on the menu.

When Tony and I came in to eat, they had run out of spaghetti sauce on the buffet line. The cook said, "Wait a minute. I got some more in the kitchen."

A minute or so later, Tony went back to the kitchen and found the guy mixing ketchup and water to make some "spaghetti sauce" for us. Tony had a fit.

Tony had a way of putting people in their place.

Once Chuck Knox was visiting the equipment room. Knox pulled out a wad of money and counted out $1,700.

"See, Tony, this is just walking around money for a head coach in the National Football League," Knox said proudly.

Tony, who never used banks, reached into his pocket and pulled out an impressive wad — $1,300.

"I've got $1,300 and I'm only a peasant", he said to Knox. "I guess being a head coach in the NFL doesn't pay much."

Knox just walked out in a huff.

The equipment room at Niagara University was one flight up and overlooked the player's locker room.

Our center Bruce Jarvis had suffered a knee injury during a Saturday night preseason game. Now it was Sunday and Jarvis had just learned that he had to have surgery on his knee and would be out for the season.

Dejected, he went to the locker room and in his frustration began throwing things –- shaving cream, bottles of after-shave lotion, deodorant — against the wall of the shower room. All the while, he was shouting "Why me, Lord? Why me?"

Marchitte, who naturally would have to clean up the mess and happened to be looking down on the scene from his second-floor perch, bellowed:

"Because, you're an asshole. That's why."

Just a couple of years after he retired, Tony died of lung cancer. During his last months, he would wait at the corner store in his neighborhood in Cheektowaga and chastise the kids who were going in to buy cigarettes.

In those early years the training and equipment staff was flying by the seat of our pants. We had to know how to do everything. When we held training camp at the Regency Hotel in Blasdell, we cut the grass on the field, lined the field, put the snow fence up to keep people out, did the laundry, shined the shoes.

If you didn't have some piece of equipment, you made do.

I remember Dick Gallagher, the general manager, once complaining that I was using too much tape. So I got the figures from the league on how much tape each team was using and I was right in the bottom third. I think I was like fifth or sixth among eight teams.

"I'm not using any more tape than anyone else," I told him.

"OK," he said, "But make sure you use it right down to the end of the roll."

That was life in the American Football League, nothing compared to the Cadillac days to come in the NFL.

After Tony Marchitte retired, Chuck Knox brought in a former Marine, Chuck Ziober, to run the equipment room. That's how tough the equipment man's job is dealing with the players – and coaches. You have to be an ex-Marine to do the job.

Dave Hojnowski, who paid his dues as an assistant under Marchitte and Ziober, took over as equipment manager. He started on the ground floor. As a high school kid he came in and helped Tony with the laundry detail. "Hojo" is still on the job and still doling out towels, jocks and wisecracks.

One of the things "Hojo" used to say about me is that I know the first lines of a thousand songs but nothing more.

He's probably right and it's probably a good thing.

"Hojo" and his assistant, Randy "Woody" Ribbeck, were a big help to me throughout the last dozen or so years I was trainer.

They call him "Woody" because he used to look like Woody Allen. Like "Hojo", Woody is from North Tonawanda High School. I guess you can call North Tonawanda the "Cradle of Equipment Men".

Woody wasn't a bad athlete himself. He can run for hours. If you've been to a Bills training camp you see him running from practice field to practice field, changing chinstraps, repairing helmets. He never stops. Woody is the guy who runs out on the field and retrieves the kicking tee after a kickoff. He still does it at full speed.

Woody used to field punts in practice and in pregame warm-ups for our kickers. He's been doing it so long, I'll bet he can catch them with his eyes closed. Some of the return men we've had aren't as sure-handed as Woody.

That reminds me of Ronnie Pitts, a former Bill who grew up around the team because his dad, the late Elijah Pitts, was an assistant coach. When Ronnie was in high school he was a ballboy in training camp. He used to come out to practice and field punts from Marv Bateman, who was our punter at the time. Sometimes, it was embarrassing. Ronnie used to punt the ball back to Bateman and actually outkick him.

Although Ronnie was a talented punter and kicked at Orchard Park High School, he never was called on to do that at UCLA. Once, I asked him why he didn't punt at UCLA.

"Nobody ever asked me," he said, modestly.

Last minute mental preparations in the locker room before a game in 1966.

CHAPTER SIX

"Lamonica, you're killing me."

The biggest problem the Bills had when Buster Ramsey was coach was quarterback. The first quarterbacks we had were Tommy O'Connell and Johnny Green. The next year, 1961, we had M.C. Reynolds and Warren Rabb. The other teams in the AFL had an advantage over us at quarterback with guys like George Blanda, Cotton Davidson, Jack Kemp, Frank Tripucka, Tom Flores, Butch Songin and Al Dorow.

Things began to change for the Bills in 1962 when Lou Saban took over as coach. That year we drafted Mike Stratton and Tom Sestak. It's also the year Cookie Gilchrist came down from Canada to play fullback. In the middle of the season we found the answer to the quarterback problem when we got Kemp on waivers from San Diego for a $100. Kemp had a broken finger and Sid Gillman, the Chargers' coach, put him on waivers, figuring nobody would take him. We claimed him for the waiver price and when the broken finger healed we had our quarterback.

Even the way Kemp's finger healed was a blessing. The joint fused itself so the finger wouldn't straighten out but it fit the shape of the football perfectly.

Kemp could throw the ball a mile. He was one of the first quarterbacks who was into weight training. A good strong guy.

One of the best trades we made was when we got Wray Carlton, a running back, in our first season. We got him from New England for Al Crow, a defensive end. Wray was a good, big running back and fit right into Lou's style of playing.

Slowly we started to put together some talent, even though there was

*Daryle Lamonica, "Golden Wheels" Dubenion and Cookie Gilchrest
share a tense moment on the bench at War Memorial Stadium.*

competition with the NFL. In 1961 we drafted and signed Billy Shaw, Stew Barber and Al Bemiller, who became the anchors for our offensive line. Harvey Johnson, in his infinite wisdom, recruited guys from areas where there were no NFL teams, like the Deep South. The Mike Strattons, the Jim Dunaways, the Billy Shaws, most of our players came from there.

Also, Saban had a knack for picking players who can switch positions and be standouts. Harry Jacobs was a guard in college at Bradley. Lou switched him to middle linebacker. John Tracey was changed from tight end to linebacker. George Saimes, one of the most prolific running backs in Michigan State history, moved to safety. Minnesota and Houston cut Ron McDole as an offensive tackle. Lou made him a defensive end and switched Tom Day to defensive end, then to guard and back to defensive end again.

Lou usually had his way at draft time.

I sat in on one meeting Lou had with our scouts. Bob Celeri, one of the scouts, was trying to convince Lou to draft a defensive back from Drake. Celeri was running through the positives of the unnamed player.

Saban listened for a while but finally ran out of patience. He was holding a pencil in his hand and snapped it like a twig.

"I don't want this guy," Lou said emphatically.

Celeri did a complete 180 without hesitating. "Well, coach, this guy does have some negatives," he said.

Needless to say, we didn't draft that guy.

We were able to sign Cookie Gilchrist because of Harvey Johnson's connections in the Canadian League. In 1962, Cookie reported in time to play in a preseason game against the New York Titans in New Haven, Conn. Right from the start, Saban had trouble figuring him out.

At halftime in that first game, Cookie came into the locker room and took off all his equipment.

Saban panicked. "What's he doing?" he asked me. "Is he quitting?"

Cookie just had this routine; he would change his T-shirt, his jock and his socks at halftime of every game. Sometimes he would shower, too.

Sometimes he wouldn't, but he would change his stuff and make it dry.

Saban was relieved to know Cookie wasn't quitting, but eventually the relationship between the two did sour.

Later in the preseason of 1962, we played the Oilers in Mobile, Ala., which was racially segregated at the time. Our main hotel was downtown, but our black players were quartered in a black hotel on the other side of town.

Before the game, I went over to the black hotel to tape the players – Cookie, Tom Day, Booker Edgerson and the others. I felt a little uncomfortable as I approached the hotel. Tom Day didn't help matters.

Standing on the hotel balcony, Day called out to a group of guys hanging out on the corner.

"Get that whitey. Get that whitey," he yelled.

I was scared until Cookie showed up.

"I'll take care of you, Eddie. Don't worry," he said.

Thank God for Cookie. Of course, after it was over, Day said, "I wouldn't let anything happen to you. You know that."

We all had a good laugh over it.

With the arrival of Saban, Cookie and finally Kemp all in the same season, we were getting better. Down the stretch in 1962 we were 7-1-1 and finished with our first winning season at 7-6-1. In 1963, we were 7-6-1 again but lost a playoff with the Boston Patriots for the Eastern Division championship. Lucky thing. After beating us, 26-8, the Patriots were demolished by the San Diego Chargers in the AFL championship game.

We weren't ready to challenge the Chargers yet, but by the next year, we were ready to make the Bills' first championship run.

The thing I'll remember about the American Football League is that there were only six championship rings before the merger with the NFL and we've got two of them. That's what I'm most proud of. We won our division three times in seven years. We beat San Diego in the championship games in 1964 and 1965, but lost to Kansas City at home in 1966 for the right to go to the first Super Bowl against the Green Bay Packers.

In my heart, I believe if we had beaten Kansas City we would have given Green Bay a much better game than the Chiefs did. Why? Because Green Bay had a good running game and we had a great run defense. I can remember in the AFL championship game, at War Memorial Stadium, we were going in for a score before halftime and Kemp got intercepted. Johnny Robinson of the Chiefs ran it back for them and set up a touchdown and we were never in the game after that.

Sweetest of all, was beating San Diego twice for the AFL championship — 20-7 in 1964 and 23-0 in 1965. We were the underdog both times.

The Chargers had that cocky air about them. They thought they were better than any other team in the league. They always came to Buffalo and acted like it was a hick town. Because of that, we had no trouble getting up to play those guys.

In the 1964 AFL championship game at War Memorial Stadium on a very muddy day, one play turned the game around. The Chargers scored first, but on their next possession, Tobin Rote, their quarterback, threw a swing pass out in the left flat to a running back, Keith Lincoln. Mike Stratton, our outside linebacker, came up and drove his shoulder into Lincoln's ribs just as the ball arrived. It was just an incomplete pass but it turned out to be a huge play. Lincoln broke three ribs on the play and had to leave the game.

It was a fantastic hit by Stratton. He just timed it perfectly. Stratton came in there and hit him the way you teach a guy to hit a blocking sled, perfect form and technique and everything else. It was totally legitimate. Lincoln was stretched out, reaching for the ball when Stratton him.

Stratton's hit lit a fire under our team. It got the guys going, and all fired up. You could feel that on the sidelines. No question. We went on to win, 20-7.

In the '65 game, we supposedly had no chance. They had murdered us, 34-6, in Buffalo and we got a tie out at Balboa Stadium when Pete Gogolak kicked a field goal in the final seconds. Not only did we beat them again for a second straight title, we shut them out, 23-0, in San

Diego. Lou came out with a two tight-end offense and we went right down the field for a touchdown in the second quarter. Kemp threw a touchdown pass to Ernie Warlick, the tight end. Warlick had a great game. Then Butch Byrd ran a punt back 74 yards for another touchdown before halftime and that totally demoralized the Chargers. Gogolak finished them off with three field goals in the second half.

One thing stands out: Booker Edgerson, our cornerback, running down the Chargers' great receiver, Lance Alworth, from behind. Not only did it save a touchdown, it also fired everyone up.

Booker never got the credit he deserved for being a good player, but I was happy to see him inducted into the Greater Buffalo Sports Hall of Fame in 2001. It was about time somebody recognized what a great player he was.

Byrd, the other corner, got all the accolades. Butch was a good player, too, but wasn't as good a cover guy as Booker. The defensive coaches used to give Byrd help in coverage and leave Booker to go by himself in man-for-man coverage.

Another thing that gave us a big lift in the 1965 championship game was George Flint filling in at left guard for Billy Shaw, who got knocked out covering the opening kickoff. All game Flint lined up across from the Big Cat, Ernie Ladd, the biggest guy in the league at 6-foot-9 and 300 pounds. Flint didn't weigh 245 pounds soaking wet, but he held his own against Ladd, just like Shaw usually did.

Flint was like Jim Ritcher, who played left guard on our four Super Bowl teams. When we had the team weigh in at training camp, he always put weights in his towel or jockstrap to boost his weight. He was always afraid the coaches would cut him because he was too light.

I had a strange episode involving Sid Gillman, the coach of the Chargers. We were in Houston for the AFL All-Star Game after the 1965 season. As the AFL champions we played against the league All-Stars. A couple days before the game I was walking outside on the grounds of our hotel and I found two checks on the ground that were made out to Gillman and were endorsed for $1,000. I wanted to return them to him so I called him and left a message at his hotel. At first, I didn't hear from him. I called him back again and this time I spoke to him. He acted like he didn't want to have anything to do with me. Finally, I told him, "I have these two checks that belong to you. If you want to meet me I want to return them to you."

Finally he agreed to meet me. He came down to the hotel. He just took the two checks and turned around and walked away, never even gave me a thank-you. I could never figure it out.

Gilchrist led our team in rushing in the 1964 championship season, but he wasn't around for 1965.

Saban had waived him in the middle of the 1964 season after he walked out on the team during a game. The players, Kemp and Shaw and all those guys, got together and went to Saban. "Lou," they said, "you always wanted us to stick together as a team. We want Cookie back."

Lou agreed to reinstate him for the rest of the season, but that was it. He told Cookie right off, "Cookie, the guys want you back, but you ain't going to be here next year. I'm only taking you back because the guys want you back."

Lou meant it. A couple of months after the season was over, he traded Cookie to Denver for Billy Joe, another fullback.

Our defense, led by Sestak and the linebackers, was dominant in 1965 and it had to be. Cookie was gone and we were low on wide receivers after we lost Elbert Dubenion and Glenn Bass with injuries early in the season. Just before the game in Kansas City in the sixth week, Lou traded Tom Keating, a young defensive tackle, to Oakland for Bo Roberson, a fast receiver. The trade was supposed to be announced after the game, so Saban decided to use Keating in the game because he was still on our roster.

Dr. Joe Godfrey, our regular orthopedist, couldn't make the trip and had sent Dr. Rainer, a resident, in his place.

On the first kickoff, Keating runs down and tears up his knee. While Keating is down on the field with Dr. Rainer and I attending to him, Lou comes out all panicky.

"What's wrong with him? What's wrong with him?" Saban says.

The doctor was afraid to tell him. I said, "Coach, I think he tore his knee up."

"It can't be. It can't be," Lou says. "I just traded him to Oakland. We've got to wait until Dr. Godfrey sees him."

Again, I said, "Coach, I think he tore his knee up."

"Well, goddammit," Lou said, "the Raiders will just have to take him in a cast."

The trade went through anyway, but it was announced that Oakland would get two players to be named later. Keating recovered and had a nice career with the Raiders.

Lou could get emotional. One game, Daryle Lamonica was playing quarterback and called the wrong formation. He went to hand the ball off and nobody was there so he ran it himself and made the first down. With the clock stopped he came over to the sidelines to get the next play from Lou. Saban was still mad because Lamonica had called the wrong formation on the play before.

"You're killing me, Lamonica. You're killing me," Lou was yelling.

"You don't know near from far, strong from weak," he said, and went on berating Daryle some more.

When he was finished Lamonica looked at him and said, "Coach, we don't have much time. What play do you want me to call? I made the first down, didn't I? Don't worry about it."

That just made Lou all the madder.

"I'm going to kill you, Lamonica," Lou said.

Another time, Daryle threw about eight or nine passes in a row and misfired on all of them. Lamonica came over to the sideline and Saban is screaming at him again.

"My God, Daryle," Lou says. "You couldn't hit the ocean if you were standing on the shore."

"Relax, Coach," Lamonica said. "I'm going to complete the next nine passes."

He caught Lou off guard for a second with that comment.

"How do you know you're going to complete the next nine passes," Lou asked.

"Because, I'm a 50 percent passer, Coach."

Once after a game in Houston, Lou was in the shower all lathered up when someone came in and told him Tex Maule, the pro football writer from Sports Illustrated,wanted to talk to him.

Maule hated the American Football League, but he was a very influential writer and Lou wanted to make himself available. Lou wrapped himself in a towel and interrupted his shower to talk with Maule.

The interview lasted about 10 minutes. All the while all the hot water was running in all the showers and sinks because the players didn't think to turn them off.

Finally, Lou went back to the shower. A moment later, there was a shriek. The water was like ice and Saban began complaining to Tony Marchitte.

Tony walked in and turned off all the faucets and said, "Lou, you have no discipline on your team. You let the players leave the water running and never complain about it to them. If you did that in your house you wouldn't have any hot water there either."

"Ok, Tony. Peace," Saban said. "I started to chew you out and I end up getting chewed out."

Once, we were playing the New York Titans at the old Polo Grounds in New York and Tom Sestak, the defensive tackle, got knocked out. He was out like a light and when we went out on the field to attend to him we found him snoring like a baby. He was out two or three minutes, a long time, but finally came to. We took him inside on a stretcher, checked his neck over. He had no residual symptoms,but he was through for that game.

The next day, he came the trainer's room back in Buffalo. I asked him, "Tom, you got a headache?"

"No," he said. "Nothing's wrong."

Dr. Godfrey had him tested anyway. His EEG (Electro Encephalogram – brain wave test) was normal so we just held him of practice for a day or two because he was chomping at the bit to go.

Another time, Tom Day, the defensive end, was down flat on his back on the field after a play. I went out with the doctor to see what the problem was.

Tippy was just lying there looking up, just using the time to take a little break.

"I'm OK," he said, "but how are the fans taking it?"

In those days, the players played mostly because they loved the game. They didn't make a lot of money and they were always worried about losing their jobs.

One year Shaw, Barber and Bemiller were holding out. They each were asking for $500 more and made a vow to stick together until all three got their raises, but Billy caved in and signed and the other guys were mad at him for a while. In the end it didn't affect their friendship, but Bemiller and Barber razzed Billy about how weak he was for the rest of the season.

Even before we won the first championship in 1964, you could see something special was building because the guys were really like a family and hung together. Lou knew how to prod them, and we had a very intelligent group of guys. Billy Shaw, Dick Hudson, Stew Barber, Al Bemiller, Ernie Warlick — they were all bright guys.

I was beginning to learn not to take anything for granted in pro football and I got another lesson only a few weeks after we beat the Chargers for the championship in 1965.

Right after the first of the year in 1966, Saban resigned to become the head coach at the University of Maryland. Joe Collier, the defensive coordinator, took over.

Lou was gone, but not for good as it turned out. Still, it would be a long time before the Bills became a championship team again.

CHAPTER SEVEN

Coaches I have known.

If it weren't for Buster Ramsey bringing me to Buffalo, I probably wouldn't be where I am today. He was the first of nine different head coaches I worked under. Of course I worked with Lou Saban and Harvey Johnson, twice each.

I've already written a lot about Buster. He was colorful and unique. Saban wasn't as colorful, but he was definitely unique.

When Saban took over in 1962, things changed a lot. Lou had an eye for talent and organization, but he spent a lot of time on dealing psychologically with the players. He worked on their psyches a lot.

When the guys were doing lousy he would pick them up. When a guy did well, that's when he would berate him.

Lou had a trick he used whenever he talked to the team. He would always stand on an equipment trunk or a bench so he would be looking down at the guys and they would have to look up at him when he was speaking.

I remember we were playing a game in Denver in the 1963 season, we were leading in the last minute and a half and the Broncos scored a touchdown. It cut the final margin to two points, 30-28. Even though we won, Lou didn't like the fact that we let Denver get that close.

After the game, as soon as all the players were in the room and the door was closed, Lou started to berate the team.

"Guys, I know we had the game won, but a good team never lets up. Never let a team up. That's the most important time in the game," he told them.

Bobby Chandler with J.D. Hill and Ahmad Rashad,
one of Buffalo's best all-time trios.

While Lou was ranting, I was cutting some tape off Billy Shaw's knees. Billy turned and looked at me with a puzzled look on his face and said, "Eddie, I thought we won this game."

One game in the early '70s, Bobby Chandler missed a pass that hit him in the facemask and bounced away. Lou always ran the projector at the team meeting on Monday when they went over the previous day's game film. When the Chandler play came up, Lou turned off the projector and said, "Turn on the lights."

"Look," he said to the team. "I don't want any of you guys bitching about Chandler missing this pass or anything. He's won a lot of games, caught a lot of balls for us. It happens."

Two weeks later, Chandler had a great game. He caught about 10 balls, and made one of those grabs where he's laid out parallel to the ground, with his toes barely in bounds and catching the ball. The next day, when the team saw the play in the film room, everybody cheered, but not Lou.

He snapped the off switch on the projector and said, "Turn on the lights."

"Chandler," he said. "You think you're a great receiver. Where were you three weeks ago when I needed you in the Dallas game?"

When Lou was in the Army during World War II he was trained to speak Mandarin Chinese. Once, when we were getting ready to play the New York Jets, he gave his pregame pep talk in Mandarin.

"Ching, yong, ming yong, yong, yong ching. . . ." Nobody knew what he was saying. The players were looking at each other thinking Saban had lost his mind.

Finally, Tom Sestak raised his hand. "What are you saying, coach?"

"I'm saying, 'beat the hell out of the Jets.' Don't you understand me?"

Then, they went out and did just that.

Lou had a way of delivering a message without confronting a player directly or embarrassing him.

There was a time when O.J. Simpson and Jim Braxton were coming out late to the practice field every day. Lou found a way to deal with that without a confrontation.

He came up to me before practice and said, "Eddie, here's what I want you to do today. Come out late to practice. Then disregard what I'm going to say to you, but I want to get a point across to a couple of guys."

"OK," I said and came out five minutes late, when the team was already practicing.

When I came out onto the field, Lou suddenly blew his whistle.

"Everybody up here," he said, calling the team together.

"Look," he said, pointing to me. "We won three games and everybody is getting complacent. Look at the trainer. He comes out here five minutes late. Yeah. That's what's happening. We're getting complacent."

He's talking about me but all the time he's looking right at O.J. and Braxton, who got the message.

Lou came up to me after practice and said, "That wasn't too bad, was it?"

"No," I said. "But all the guys are giving me crap. They're saying, 'Hey, Big Time, Coach is on your ass. It's nice he's on your ass, for a change, instead of ours.' "

I told them, "I could handle it. I've got big shoulders."

I became a pretty good pinochle player thanks to Lou. During the offseason he and the late Pat McGroder, the team vice president, used to come down to the training room at lunch hour to play cards. Tony Marchitte and I won a lot of lunch money from those guys.

Lou left after the 1965 championship season and Joe Collier, the defensive coordinator, took over. Collier epitomized that old Leo Durocher line about nice guys finishing last. He was one of the brightest coaches you'd ever want to see and is a very dear friend to this day. When Pat and I moved into our new house, Joe and his wife came over and welcomed us to the neighborhood.

He was such a good guy; he would never put the blame on the players. He always took the blame. If we got beat bad, he would come into the locker room and he'd say, "Guys, I must not have prepared you well because I know you aren't that bad."

Once we were playing Oakland in our stadium and getting beat really bad at halftime. Joe came in and started apologizing to the players, as usual. Richie McCabe, who had taken over the defense when Joe moved up to head coach, interrupted him.

"Joe, excuse me," Richie said. "Would you leave the room for a few minutes?"

When Collier left, Richie really lit into the guys. "You're going to get us all fired," he told the players. "But you know something: I'm going to be coaching in this league somewhere and some of you guys are going to be put on waivers and I'm going to have a say in whether you play again or not. If anybody asks me about you guys, I'm going to say you're phony baloney."

Richie really laid into them. The result was we had a really good second half but we had just too many points to make up and lost the game, 24-20.

Collier always looked at the good side of the guys. I remember once telling him that one of the players wasn't coming to the training room for injury treatment like he was supposed to.

Joe just shrugged and said, "He must have a reason. He wouldn't do that without a reason. I'll talk to the guy."

The player came in the next day and apologized to me but there were no repercussions. The upshot was, Joe didn't do anything. He was just too nice a guy.

Collier and McCabe were two of the brightest football guys here, in my opinion. When Richie was a playing as a defensive back he would call the plays Buster's offense would be running in scrimmages before the ball was snapped. He could tell just by just by looking at the formation, the way guys were leaning and other things.

"Watch the run wide, or they're going to run a hook here," he would yell out. It would drive Buster crazy and he finally would tell Richie to get off the field and sit on the bench and watch.

Richie kept his own playbook; the thing was three times the size of what the other players had. When he was playing we had Jimmy Wagstaff, Billy Kinard and Billy Atkins with him in the secondary. None of them wanted to play cornerback. Richie volunteered to play corner even though he had been a safety for the Washington Redskins in the NFL and weighed only 168 pounds. He had such football savvy; he would look at a play on the film projector and in two swipes could tell you what all 11 guys did. He always did his own film breakdown. He wouldn't accept other people's work.

Richie had three stints with us, one as a player and two as an assistant coach. After he left the Bills the third time, he was coaching in Denver, where he died of colon cancer. It was a really sad day for me because we really watched him closely here. Owen Bossman, one of our team doctors, always made Richie come in for checkups. If he had anything wrong with him, he would always tell me. He was very private, though. I guess when he went to Denver he didn't tell anybody on their medical staff there was anything wrong with him until it was too late.

A knee injury ended Richie's playing career with the Bills. When he hurt the knee, Buster wanted him to hang around, but Richie refused. "I don't need this thing. I don't want to take your money. I'm going home." And he went home, although he later came back as an assistant coach with Saban.

The day he left, he came in the training room and handed me twenty dollars. Back then, the guys paid three or five dollars clubhouse dues to Tony Marchitte and me for shining their shoes and all that stuff.

He said, "Here, this is for you for the extra time you spent with me. Take Pat and the kids out for dinner."

I said "No," but he threw it on the floor. That was the type of person he was. He apologized for making me work so hard with his knee.

"I should have just hung it up at the beginning of the year and that was it," he said.

Richie was a good coach. He took Charlie Romes, who had played only one year of college football — he was a trackman — and made him into a good DB. He took Robert James, who was a defensive end at Fisk University, and made him into an All-Pro cornerback.

When Collier got fired after the second game of the 1968 season, all the assistant coaches went in asking for the job. Not Richie. He went in and said to Ralph Wilson, "I was in charge of the defense. We sucked. You've got to fire me."

As it turned out, Ralph kept him and the other guys left.

Harvey Johnson took over as the interim coach when Collier was fired. He didn't want the job. He was happy being the college scout, but out of loyalty to Ralph he took over the team. Of course, Ralph insisted. Three years later, when John Rauch was fired as head coach in training camp before the start of the 1971 season, Harvey knew he was going to get the call again. He tried hiding from Ralph in the training room, trying to avoid the call, but he couldn't get away with it.

I can't say I enjoyed the two years when Rauch was head coach. The team was losing and Rauch was suspicious of everybody in the organization except people he brought in.

Rauch was a hard guy to get to know and get close to. I think he was paranoid after working for Al Davis in Oakland for so long. Everything was secretive with him.

Rauch was an insecure guy. He used to make the trainers and doctors leave the locker room before he made his pregame talk to the team. He'd had some run-ins with Dr. Godfrey about medical problems, and I didn't think he liked the way it was handled, so he didn't trust the medical department.

Of course, Rauch is always remembered in Buffalo for misusing O.J. Simpson. For two seasons, he used him mostly as a decoy, or a pass receiver or on kickoff returns.

When Lou Saban came in, he told O.J., "You're going to carry the ball 30 times a game. Is that OK with you?" And that was it.

After Saban quit as head coach the second time in the middle of the 1976 season, Jim Ringo, who had been the offensive line coach, took over.

Ringo was very intense, a good guy but very impatient with people.

We had a defensive lineman named Steve Okoniewski who was a good player but was very slow because he was splayfooted. This frustrated Ringo. He asked the doctor if it were possible to break Okoniewski's feet and reset them straight so he would be able to run faster. I don't know if he was serious or not.

Ringo used to follow my weight battle with interest. One June, I lost 25 pounds.

Jim came to the training room one day and said, "Oh my God, Eddie, you've lost weight again. Since I've known you you've lost 400 pounds. You shouldn't exist."

As far as I was concerned, Ringo was a trainer's dream because he wouldn't let the guys come in to the training room with piddling injuries. When he was offensive line coach, he would bring all his linemen in at the start of training camp and introduce them to me.

"Now, this is the trainer's room," he'd say. "I don't want anybody coming in here for any little nicks and bruises. When you come in here you have to have something serious."

All the guys used to tell me that in the first year any bruises they had they used to treat themselves in their dorm room and not say anything about it because they were afraid Ringo would think they weren't tough enough. They wanted to make the team so badly they wouldn't complain if they had a charley horse or a sore calf muscle, injuries they could play with.

Despite some differences with Rauch, Dr. Godfrey stayed on as the team doctor, but when Chuck Knox became head coach and took over football operations in 1978, Dr. Godfrey was replaced by Dick Weiss.

All the successful coaches we had were very good as far as the medical staff was concerned. They let us do our job, more or less. All the coaches who tried to intervene were unsuccessful. With Marv Levy and Lou Saban, if the medical department said you couldn't play, you couldn't play. They didn't say I've got to have him or I need him or it's got to be this or that.

Even though he wasn't successful in Buffalo, Hank Bullough, to me, was a terrific coach for the training staff because he made those guys toe the mark. Whenever I told him anything, he followed through on it. He was up there with Lou and Marv as far as being good to trainers.

Those coaches, whenever you told them a player wasn't going to be there on Sunday, they just accepted whatever we said.

"OK, we'll work with this guy or we'll work with that guy," they would say. Or "Whatever we have that's what we got them for." And they would coach whoever was there.

When you have that kind of confidence in what you're doing as a medical department you really try hard to get the guys ready to play.

I saw a lot of different assistant coaches come through Buffalo. Dick Jauron, who later became the head coach of the Chicago Bears, was here for one year. I knew he would be a head coach someday because he was a really intelligent guy.

Tom Catlin, the defensive coordinator under Chuck Knox, was another good coach. The three smartest defensive coaches I ever knew were Catlin, Richie McCabe and Joe Collier.

Monte Kiffin, who later became the defensive coordinator with Tampa Bay, was a great guy. He was all football. He would never talk about anything but football. It consumed his life. I never once heard him say the weather is nice, or what about the Yankees or let's do this or let's do that.

One of the guys Rauch brought in and one of the few he seemed to trust was Bugsy Engleberg (his real name was Lewis) who was more of a personal assistant for Rauch than a coach. I don't think the Bills knew Rauch was bringing him with him. He was really the gopher for Rauch, although he was supposed to be in charge of the kickers.

One year, we brought this guy in from the Canadian League to kick. He could kick the ball off deep, but he was a little erratic with his placekicking. Bugsy started tutoring him every day. The guy's field goal kicking didn't get any better after Bugsy got through coaching him, and instead of kicking the ball deep into the end zone on kickoffs, it got to where he could only reach the goal line. Pretty soon he was barely reaching the 5-yard line and then the 10.

The guy was getting frustrated. Finally, Bugsy said to him: "You'd better go back to your old style."

"I can't remember what it was," the kid said. Bugsy had changed him so many times, had him so screwed up, he ended up getting cut.

Tony Marchitte used to play gin rummy with Bugsy every day and get us extra meal money for the road. We'd eat free on Bugsy or Tony used to take the money and go out and buy himself socks, ties or underwear. Then he'd taunt Bugsy.

"Hey, Bugsy," he'd say. "Got me three pair of shorts today on you," or "Look at this nice tie you bought me, Bugsy."

Tony would never let up on the poor guy.

Of course, Marv Levy had more success than any coach we had. Marv didn't bother the training staff much or hang around the training room, although he would come in every day after he had gone for his run or after a workout.

Marv always had great jokes. Cute jokes, nothing off color. We always talked about World War II or books he had read.

He used to tell the story about the animals on Noah's Ark having a football game. One side got way behind, and in the second half, the centipede got in the game and ran wild. In what was probably the first Monday morning quarterbacking ever, Noah asked the coach why the centipede didn't play in the first half.

"Because he spent the whole first half lacing his shoes," came the response.

That was an example of Marv's understated dry humor.

CHAPTER EIGHT

The amazing Sestak and others giants from the AFL years

If you asked me my favorites among the hundreds of Bills players I worked with over the years, I wouldn't give you an answer. There were too many of them and I'd probably leave somebody out.

On the other hand, though, there are players who were just too prominent to ignore and a lot of good times that I can't overlook.

Jack Kemp

Long before he became a congressman or ran for vice president, Jack used to run his political philosophies by me. We used to get into a lot of discussions.

When he first started in politics, I tried to explain to him that he had to get more in the middle of the curve and away from the extremes. The guys on either end don't get elected; they don't get enough votes, I told him.

One time we were having a discussion about Social Security.

"Do we really need Social Security?" he asked for the sake of argument. "My dad doesn't need it."

I said, "Hey, all I know is my dad worked in the steel mill and the most he ever made was $3,200 a year. We never even owned a car."

"My dad owned a trucking company," he said.

"How much did your dad earn a year," I asked him. He said, "$39,000."

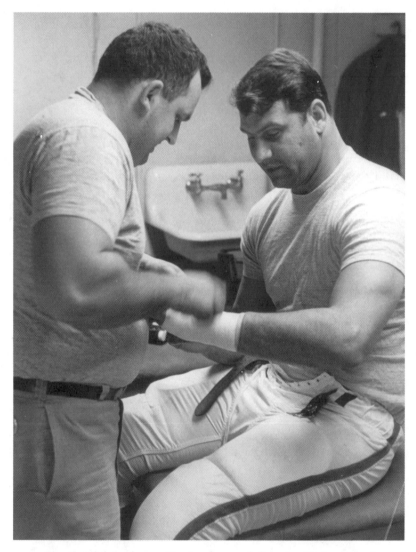

Here I am helping the great Tom Sestak get ready for action. "Ses" was one of the most amazing Bills and deserves to be in the Pro Football Hall of Fame.

I said, "If my dad made $39,000 he wouldn't need Social Security either."

He was always giving me stuff to read. Once, he gave me the book, "The Rise and Fall of the Roman Empire."

I don't know how smart he is, but Jack was the best-read man I ever met. I voted for him every time he ran for office even though I didn't necessarily agree with everything he believed in. That's how much I respected him.

If ever Kemp became president, I always thought to myself what a big thrill it would be to be able to get on the phone and call the president and say "this is Eddie. I want to tell you something".

I'm sure he'd take my call because he's that kind of guy. We had a really good relationship.

Harry Jacobs

Our two AFL championship teams had a couple of Rodney Dangerfield guys who didn't get the respect they deserved. One was Booker Edgerson, at cornerback. The other guy like that was Harry Jacobs, who never got noticed because he was just so steady and reliable. We never saw him in the training room. He just played every week.

Harry called all the defenses for the Bills. In those days the coaches did not signal in the defensive calls from the sidelines as they do now. Richie McCabe once told me that he would go over the game plan with Harry and what defenses they wanted him to call, depending on the situation. Ninety-seven percent of the time, Richie said, Harry called the right defense with no help from the sidelines.

Tom Sestak

Tom Sestak, who was a defensive tackle on the Bills' AFL championship teams in 1964 and 1965, was one of the top players I've ever been around. I spent five years with the Lions and saw them all — — Joe Schmidt, Alex Karras, Wayne Walker, Darris McCord, Lou Creekmur, Bobby Layne, John Gordy, Yale Lary, Jack Christiansen. I always thought Sestak should be in the Pro Football Hall of Fame. He was one tough dude. He didn't get the fame he should have received because he never had the chance to go against the NFL teams in the prime of his career.

"Ses" made the All-AFL team his next-to-last year of playing even though he never practiced with the team because of his bad knees. All he did each day during practice was ride a stationary bike, his knee was so bad. He was just a super guy. It was amazing how well he played considering how bad his knees were. His tolerance to pain was legendary.

Once he came into the training room and said, "Doc, my back is bothering me."

It turned out he got kicked in the back two weeks before.

I said, "Why didn't you say anything?"

"I thought it was going away," he said.

I sent him to St. Mary's Hospital to get X-rayed. The report came back: "Three broken ribs — healing nicely."

He never missed a practice or a game. That was Tom Sestak.

Stew Barber

I don't remember what year it was, but one season he had a fractured cheekbone. It was a depression fracture, but he was able to play with it. After the game, we would take him to Mercy Hospital and they would pop the cheekbone back into place. The first time he stayed in the hospital overnight and checked out the next day. The next week he played and it popped out again. He went back to the hospital, but this time he refused to stay. It happened a third time and he walked out of the hospital again after the surgeons finished putting the bone back in place. The nuns at Mercy were all upset, but there was no way they were going to make Stew spend another night in the hospital.

Billy Shaw

Billy had knee surgery in 1967. He was supposed to be out for eight

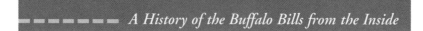

*One of my proudest moments, presenting Billy Shaw
for his induction into the Pro Football Hall of Fame.*

weeks. He was ready in six. After surgery in those days, the first thing you had to do when the cast came off was get range of motion back in the joint. Then you could start using weights to build up the muscle. Billy worked on getting his range of motion back on his own. He used to do leg lifts with his little daughter sitting on his foot. Because of his determination, he easily beat the time schedule for his recovery.

I remember one game when Billy came to the sidelines with a pulled hamstring muscle. We thought he was through for the game because of the pain he was in.

"It only hurts when I run full-out. I'll run three-quarter speed and I'll be OK," he said. So, he decided to tough it out and went back in and finished the game, but the next day his leg was black and blue from his butt down to his knee. Still, he didn't miss any games or any practice time.

He was a super guy. That's why I was so honored when he asked me to be his presenter when he went into the Pro Football Hall of Fame in 1999. He was the first player who played his entire career in the AFL to make it to the Hall.

When Billy first called me, I tried to convince him to ask somebody else. I was never comfortable speaking in front of big crowds, even though I had forced myself to take a couple of speech courses at Purdue to get over it. When Billy called, my wife, Pat, was standing nearby. Right away she sensed what Billy wanted and when she heard me hesitating she got real animated.

"You ARE going to do it," she insisted, mouthing the words to me while I was on the phone.

So, I did it. I never would have been able to get through it if it weren't for her. I wrote my own speech (which is reprinted in the back of this book) because I wanted to be familiar with what I was saying and not be repeating what somebody else had written. I practiced that speech for three months, making sure I didn't go over the allotted four minutes, yet still did justice to Billy.

When it finally was time to get up and present Billy, I looked out at the audience and where Pat was sitting. I just kept my eyes on her and nobody else as I spoke. She had a smile on her face all the while, a smile that told me, "You're doing fine. You're doing fine."

I was the first — I think I'm still the only — trainer to act as a presenter at an enshrinement in Canton. It's something I'm proud of.

In the weeks leading up to that day, I got a lot of calls from friends in the training profession.

"The pressure's on you," they were all saying. "Represent us well."

I think I succeeded, but I'm still no great orator.

The year after Billy went into the Hall of Fame, he returned for the enshrinement of the next class and to enjoy a relaxed tour of the Hall and its displays. He was dressed casually with a baseball cap on.

When he got to where his bust was on display, there was a couple from Buffalo looking at it. The guy was telling his wife about Billy and what a great player he was. He didn't know that the real Billy Shaw was standing right next to him.

Then the guy turns around, takes the camera that was hanging from his neck and asks Billy if he would take a picture of him and his wife next to Billy Shaw's bust.

Billy did, never letting on who he was.

Jim Dunaway

Another guy who never complained about injuries was Jim Dunaway, the big defensive tackle on our championship teams in the '60s.

"Abro, that smarts," is the only thing he would say when he was hurt. Guys like that you had to hold out of practice, rather than force them into practice. That gradually changed the older I got and as the game kept changing.

Dunaway was always fighting a weight problem. He was a legendary eater. Once there was a promotion going on at Rusch's, a restaurant ... down in Dunkirk on the Lake Erie shore. They advertised all the lobster dainties you could eat for $2.95.

One night Dunaway and Ron McDole, another big eater, decided to take them up on the offer. They each put away 84 lobster dainties. That was the end of that promotion.

When they asked for the check, the manager of the restaurant, disgusted, came over and asked:

"Well, are you going to have any dessert?"

Dunaway already had his fill, but he wasn't about to let the manager get the best of him.

"What is it?" Dunaway asked.

"Strawberry shortcake," the manager replied.

"I'll take two," Dunaway said.

One year Jim came into training camp weighing over 300 pounds. He asked me to put him on a diet. I recommended an eating schedule for him. He came back a few days later and when I put him on the scale, I found he had actually gained weight.

Exasperated, I asked him, "What did you eat."

"Exactly what you told me, " Dunaway said. "Orange juice, cereal, bananas and skim milk."

McDole was standing by, taking it all in.

"Yeah," he said. "He had a quart of orange juice, the whole box of cereal in a mixing bowl, a half-gallon of milk and a whole bunch of bananas."

So much for that diet.

Cookie Gilchrist

When Cookie reported to us for the first time for a preseason game against the New York Titans in New Haven, he showed up for the bus trip wearing a white shirt, white walking shorts, white knee socks, white patent leather shoes, a red ascot and carrying a walking cane. Before Lou saw Cookie's outfit, Harvey Johnson advised Gilchrist that a less fashionable outfit might be more appropriate. So Cookie went back up and changed.

Cookie was impressive looking in uniform or out. He stood 6-2 and weighed 240 pounds. He had a 52-inch chest and a 31-inch waistline. He ran a 4.6 in the 40-yard dash. Although he was a running back, he probably would have been even more devastating as a linebacker. In fact, he once offered to play both running back and linebacker if the Bills would pay him two salaries. "I'm better than anything you've got," Cookie boasted, referring to the Bills' linebackers. He probably was. He was that complete a player. He also kicked off and kicked field goals.

Cookie did some awesome things on the field. During his time with the Bills our rivalry with the Boston Patriots got pretty intense. There was even a little hatred.

In one game against the Patriots, Cookie carried the ball around end. Defensive back Chuck Shonta was in his way. Instead of trying to put a move on Shonta, Cookie deliberately ran over him, knocking him out cold.

After they carried Shonta off, Cookie went over to the Patriots' defensive huddle and, pointing his finger, asked:

"Which one of you mothers is next?"

There were no volunteers.

Wray Carlton

Getting Wray in a trade with the Boston Patriots was one of the best trades the Bills made in their early years.

He was a strong, dependable running back who was used a lot as an outlet receiver.

Jack Kemp used to throw a lot of swing passes to Carlton in the flat. If the defense was expecting it and Ray saw he was going to get nailed and take a loss in the bargain, he used to just bat the ball down like blocking a basketball shot.

I mentioned before how Harvey Johnson used to draft players from southern schools. Another thing about Harvey, he always found intelligent players. Maybe there was no psychological and aptitude testing then, but Harvey found the guys who could succeed. We had very intelligent guys, Shaw, Hudson, Barber, Bemiller, Warlick, Carlton. They weren't guys who took basket weaving at school.

Ron McDole

"Dancing Bear" was one of the stalwarts of our AFL championship teams, then he finished his career with George Allen's Over the Hill Gang in Washington. We let him go because Johnny Rauch, in his infinite wisdom, thought McDole was washed up or else Rauch was so insecure he didn't want any of the old Bills around.

While they were playing in Buffalo, McDole and Al Bemiller started a construction company. They had built some homes in Amherst and now they wanted to build a Colonial-style home. I agreed to get the financing and they built a home for Pat and me. Part of the deal was that before we moved in we would allow them to use it as a show house for three months to promote other sales. After that they would customize it with features we wanted and we would move in. Ronnie made all the changes we asked for. We liked the house so much we never left. It's where we still live today.

Paul Maguire

Maguire was a great punter and a pretty good special teams player. In college, at The Citadel, he had been an All-Southern Conference receiver. He became such a distraction late in his career with the Bills that John Rauch actually banned him from practicing with the other players.

Maguire managed to make a general pest of himself in practice. He would always be laughing and joking like a kid in school. He seemed to have no respect for Rauch. He would mimic his voice and actions. When he was off to the side practicing his punting, he would occasionally kick the ball onto the middle of the field where the offense and defense were going through their stuff. I swear he was trying to drop a punt on top of Rauch's head. Maybe not, because Paul was such an accurate punter he probably could have hit his target if he wanted.

Maguire would come to the old Amherst Rec Center late in the morning for his punting practice and go home before the rest of the team went on the field.

I never heard of that, a player getting the afternoons off.

Maguire had an agile mind and one time his quick thinking actually helped the team.

In a preseason game against the Chicago Bears in Cleveland 1969, the center snapped the ball over his head. Maguire was chasing after the ball along with the Bears special teams. Maguire got to it first and with his back to the line of scrimmage kicked the ball backwards over his head. It rolled about 30 yards before the Bears caught up to it. He probably saved us 40 yards on the play.

After it was over, Maguire said to the center, "Geez, Pal, don't make it so hard on me."

George Saimes

He was a great running back at Michigan State but under Saban became a great safety. He was on the all-time American Football League team.

He was probably the best open-field tackler I've ever seen. One year, according to the defensive coaches, he had a chance to make 127 tackles and made 124. He only missed three tackles all season.

Saimes was an unusual guy. He was way ahead of his time in a lot of respects. A lot of things about him were unique. He was a disciple of Edgar Cayce, the psychic. He used to wash his hair with motor oil once every two weeks because he was always afraid of going bald.

He was into eating sunflower seeds. Once when the team was staying in San Diego, the maid came down to me.

"Are you in charge?" she asked me.

I asked her what the problem was.

"We've got a little bastard in room 304 and he's eating sunflower seeds and spitting them on the floor, and my vacuum cleaner won't pick them up. I have to pick them up by hand."

She was talking about George.

George's father was a shoemaker in Canton, Ohio, and George had a shoe fetish. He wore a size 8 1/2 EEEE, which is almost as wide as it is long. I had to have shoes made special for him before every season.

Saimes did everything scientifically. He would study the films of each opponent carefully. If the next opponent ran more than it passed, for that game he would wear a sturdier set of shoulder pads and a facemask with bars for the running game. If the opponent was a team that passed a lot, he would travel lighter. He would wear undersized pads and a helmet with just one bar.

Paul Costa

Paul Costa came out of Notre Dame, where he had played fullback and finally offensive tackle. Lou Saban made him a tight end.

Costa was probably the strongest player we ever had. Tremendous arm strength. After practice, he used to go out for a few beers with Maguire and Sestak. Whatever tavern they went to, Maguire would bet beers that there was nobody in the house who could beat Costa at arm-wrestling. Costa always won, so Maguire and the guys usually drank for free. He was their meal ticket.

Probably the most impressive demonstration of Costa's strength was one day when Tony Marchitte was trying to repair a shoulder harness for a player. Tony couldn't disassemble the brace because there were two metal rivets holding it together.

He tried every tool in his equipment room, with no luck. Finally, he spotted Costa walking by and asked him to help.

Costa took the brace in his hands and popped both rivets like there was nothing to it.

Tony and Doc Weiss just looked on with amazement.

Remi Prudhomme

Remi was a Cajun from Louisiana with some unusual eating habits. His pregame meal was raw meat.

Another guy who had an unusual pregame routine was Bo Roberson, a wide receiver on our 1965 team. Bo's pregame meal? A bowl of vanilla ice cream covered with honey. That's all.

Of course, there's Tom Rychlec. He was a tight end from little American International College in Massachusetts. I first ran across him when he played with the Detroit Lions. Then he came to Buffalo. Rychlec used to eat glass and worms just to prove to his teammates how wacky he was. We already knew.

Pete Gogolak

He was the first soccer-style kicker in pro football and the kicker on our two AFL championship teams.

With Gogolak, the kicking tee on kickoffs had to be placed a yard back of the 40-yard line. That's because with his kicking style, his left foot would have been ahead of the ball when he kicked and he would have been offside.

Gogolak became a historical figure in pro football. When the New York Giants signed him away from the Bills in 1966 the talent war between the leagues intensified. It got to the point that the AFL and NFL finally agreed to the pro football merger.

What I remembered about Gogolak was his mantra when he was warming up on the sidelines, when a field goal chance was coming up.

"Ten-ten, two seconds left. ... 10-10, 2 seconds left" ...he kept saying to himself over and over.

Finally one day, I asked him:

"How come it's always 10-10, 2 seconds left? How come we're never losing? Why don't you put some real pressure on yourself?"

He looked at me like I was nuts. But then kickers were always strange anyway.

Booth Lusteg

Speaking of eccentric kickers, Gogolak's replacement was Booth Lusteg, a minor league veteran from the New Bedford Sweepers of the Atlantic Coast League. Lusteg got off to a decent start with the Bills in 1966, but then started to have some problems in the middle of the season. He missed three field goals in a loss to our archrivals, the Boston Patriots, at War Memorial Stadium. That had some fans upset. To make it worse, he struggled the next week against the hated San Diego Chargers. The Bills came back from a 17-0 halftime deficit to tie the game.

We had a chance to win in the final minute on a late drive. We maneuver the ball to the middle of the field to set Lusteg up for a straight-on kick for the game- winner with six seconds left. It was only a 23-yard try, almost like an extra point, but Lusteg missed it. Wide right. Sound familiar?

Some fans were really upset. That night, Lusteg was walking near the corner of Main and Allen streets in downtown Buffalo, heading to his apartment. A carload of young guys recognized Lusteg as they drove by. They were so mad about the missed field goal, they stopped the car and beat up Lusteg.

Even though they roughed him up pretty good, Lusteg declined to press charges.

"I had it coming to me," he said.

The next week Lusteg hit all four of his attempts in a victory over Joe Namath and the New York Jets but by the end of the season, the Bills had enough.

When the 1967 season opened, Lusteg was gone. Mike Mercer was our new kicker.

1964 AFL East All Star Team.

*Tony Marchitte earning his $3 per week clubhouse
dues cleaning players' cleats after a muddy game.*

Kent Hull and Will Wolford -- the brains behind our offensive line during our glory years.

Tony Marchitte's retirement party with a collection of some of Buffalo's best.

They've seen it all – gathered in Tampa prior to Super Bowl XXV were (from left): Assistant Trainer Bud Carpenter, Joe Ferguson, Jack Kemp, Jim Kelly and Eddie Abramoski.

Sidelines during the sixties with future politician Ed Rutkowski.

Abe going on the Bills Wall of Fame in 1999.

My wife Pat and Ralph Wilson trying to figure out something nice to say about me.

CHAPTER 9

More stories on some unforgettable Bills

O. J. Simpson

Regardless of what happened later in his life, I had nothing but fond memories of the O.J. Simpson I knew in the nine seasons he spent with the Bills.

I was always amazed by the patience he showed in dealing with the media during the 1973 season, when he was on his way to breaking the 2,000-yard mark in rushing. The last month of the season, he answered the same questions from reporters day after day without losing it.

"Why don't you just tape record your answers and play the tape when the reporters come around," I suggested.

O.J. was always a friend to me and went out of his way to be generous. He always gave me money at Christmas time.

"Here," he'd say, "get something for your kids."

Whenever I was in a restaurant and he was there, he picked up the tab. When Tony Marchitte and I would go to pay the bill, the waiter or waitress would usually say "Mr. Simpson took care of that for you."

On the other hand he probably borrowed 50 quarters a year to use in the candy machine and never gave them back.

One day when I was going home from work I passed O.J. on the New York Thruway. He had been stopped for speeding by a trooper and was pulled over to the side of the road. A few minutes later, O.J. went speeding by me on his way again. It wasn't long before I went by him again. A second trooper had stopped him for speeding. I never saw

*Joe Ferguson demonstrated his courage many numerous
times during his 12-year career with the Bills.*

anybody get stopped twice for speeding on the same 20-minute trip, except O.J.

Simpson drove so fast that his buddy Reggie McKenzie threatened to wear his football helmet when he rode with him. In 1969, we played Dick Butkus and the Chicago Bears in the first game of a preseason doubleheader at the old Cleveland Stadium. The Browns and Green Bay Packers played the second game.

Before the game, Simpson asked that none of the offensive linemen do anything to piss off Butkus.

During the pregame warm-up, Simpson exchanged greetings with Butkus — very politely.

"How are things going today Mr. Butkus," Juice asked very politely.

I don't think it helped much.

Joe Ferguson

To me he was really an underrated football player. He caught the wrath of a lot of Buffalo people because he hung his head all the time, but he was such a perfectionist.

As hard as he threw the football, he never had a sore arm, never had anything wrong with his arm when he was with the Bills. He would go out there and throw it. He and Bobby Chandler, or whoever the receivers were, would stay out after practice for so long throwing balls to one another and working on timing. We would have to call them in or else they would stay out there until it was dark.

One of the greatest demonstrations of courage was put on by Ferguson at the end of the 1980 season. He had what is known today as a high-ankle sprain. He got hurt in a game at New England the next-to-last week of the regular season. The next week we had to play at San Francisco, against a 49ers team coached by Bill Walsh, with Joe Montana in his first season as the starting quarterback.

It was the season before the 49ers upset Dallas in the NFC championship game and went on to win the Super Bowl. In 1980, the Niners were just starting to show signs of being a good team.

We were leading the AFC East, but everything was riding on the San Francisco game. Win and we would be division champions and in the playoffs. Lose and we would be out of the playoffs and everything we had accomplished that year would go down the drain.

Fergy wasn't able to practice all week but we taped him up on Sunday and hoped the ankle would hold up. We got lucky. The field at Candlestick Park was very muddy and slippery that day, so the pass rushers couldn't get good traction. It was so bad each team missed an extra point on the treacherous footing. On the other hand, because it was so soft and spongy it wasn't hard on Fergy's ankle.

Ferguson threw an early touchdown pass to Jerry Butler and was just effective enough to allow us to win, 18-13. We got a safety in the third quarter for a five-point lead. That forced the Niners to have to go for six points on their last possession. Mario Clark, one of our cornerbacks, knocked down a pass in the end zone on the last play of the game to give us the victory and we were off to the playoffs.

Fergy's ankle wasn't much better for the playoff game two weeks later in San Diego. Even though we had beaten the Chargers in San Diego earlier in the season, they had home field for the playoffs because of the tiebreaker rules.

The week before the game Chuck Knox took us to Dodgertown in Vero Beach, Fla., to get out of the snow and wind in Buffalo and prepare for the warm weather in San Diego.

The ankle held up all week, but still we had our fingers crossed. As powerful an offensive team as the Chargers were with Dan Fouts, John Jefferson, Charlie Joiner and Kellen Winslow, their pass rush was pretty good - Big Hands Johnson, Fred Dean on the outside and big Louie Kelcher in the middle. They led the league in sacks that year.

Despite all their firepower, we got the Chargers locked into another defensive duel just like in our regular season meeting, when we came from 12 points down in the fourth quarter to beat them, 26-24.

This time we were hanging on to a 14-13 lead in the last five minutes of the game. Fouts nearly cost them the game when he hit Charley Romes, our other cornerback, in the numbers with a pass down the left sideline. Romes couldn't hold on, however.

A few plays later they lined up a receiver named Ron Smith in the slot, got him matched up on one of our safeties, Bill Simpson, and Fouts hit him with a 50-yard pass for the winning touchdown with 2:08 left.

Fergy was hobbling on the bad ankle by now and tried to bring us back. We got to midfield before the Chargers intercepted and were able to run out the clock.

John Holland

He was a wide receiver who played for us in the mid 1970s. John had a stuttering problem. He also loved to sing. When he sang he had no problems with stuttering, but when he was nervous he would stutter and stammer in normal conversation.

Late in one game, Lou Saban began using wide receivers to send in plays from the sidelines to the huddle. Without thinking he grabbed Holland by the shirt, gave him the play call and sent him on the field. When Holland got to the huddle, Joe Ferguson, the quarterback, was waiting for Holland to tell him the play Saban wanted to call. Holland started stuttering and just couldn't get the words out. Meanwhile the game clock was ticking down.

Finally, J.D. Hill, the other wide receiver, said: "Sing the f—— thing." And he did. "Forty-seven pass on three," he sang in beautiful tones.

Jim Haslett

You have telephones, telegrams and television. We used to have what we called "Tele-Has." The guy who now coaches the New Orleans Saints was the biggest locker room gossip. If you wanted to spread the word about something, all you had to do was whisper it to Haslett and everybody on the team would know about it in no time flat.

You could tell Haslett would be a coach someday. He was a gym rat. He was always at the stadium, in season or out, working out or just hanging around talking. You'd get to work at seven in the morning and Haslett would be there. He was a cutup when he was younger but he was really interested in football and studied it.

Fred Smerlas

Fred was Haslett's buddy. The big meatball from Boston College. I used to call Smerlas and Mark Roopenian, another defensive lineman from Boston College, "World-ologists." Those guys know everything about anything and everything. There wasn't a subject they didn't know about.

In Smerlas's senior year at Boston College the football team was 0-11.

I can't imagine him grumbling through an 0-11 season.

Whenever Smerlas would start arguing with me about football, all I had to say was:

"You were on an 0-11 team. What do you know about football?"

That would shut him up every time.

Smerlas had the messiest locker of any player who ever played for Buffalo. It was piled with old sweatsuits, unread mail, and the bags, wrappers and remains of all the fast food he used to eat.

Defensive end Sherman White used the locker next to Fred. White collected football shoes. He would never throw any of his old shoes out.

During those years we had a mouse in the locker room, which never was caught. The joke was that the mouse dined in Smerlas' locker but would never live there because it was too messy. When he finished eating he would go back next door to White's locker.

Will Grant

Will was the center on our playoff teams in the early '80s. Later on he played in a replacement game for us against the New York Giants in 1987 during the players' strike. Lawrence Taylor was playing for the Giants and nobody could handle him.

During the game, Will was called for a fifth holding penalty trying to keep LT from killing our quarterback.

After the fifth penalty, Will came to the sideline and Marv Levy exploded at him.

"Will, you're killing us. It's your fifth 10-yard penalty," Marv said.

Will looked him right in the eye and said: "Hey, coach. That ain't bad because I'm holding him on every play."

Later, he said to me: "Eddie, I can't block the son of a bitch. I had to do something. I knew the referees wouldn't call two in a row on you."

Donnie Walker

He was a defensive back with our team in the early 1970s. He came into the training room one day complaining that he was feeling ill.

"I ate some soup and I'm allergic to seafood," he told me.

"What did it say on the can?" I asked him.

"Clam chowder. I thought that was a brand name."

That reminds me of a rookie linebacker we had who was pretty talented but a little naive. One day, he asked me, "Mr. Abe, how does a thermos bottle know when to be hot and when to be cold?"

"Easy," I told him. "There's a little switch on the bottom that goes from hot to cold like a light switch."

Ben Williams

Ben was a solid defensive end for us in the late 1970s and early 1980s.

Late in his career, I was taping him before practice one day and he was still pretty beat up from playing the Sunday before and not really up to it.

"I'm doing a Nolan Ryan today," he confessed to me.

"What's a Nolan Ryan?" I asked.

"A no-hitter, man. I ain't hitting a soul."

And he didn't. He saved it for the next Sunday.

Steve Freeman

He was an undersized, but tough safetyman for us in the late 70s and '80s. He was also a very honest, hard-working guy. Now he's an official in the NFL. Tough as Steve was, I never heard him utter a swear word.

Once I was treating him for a pretty serious muscle injury. He was coming in every day for treatment but it was a bad bruise and wasn't responding very well.

Finally, Steve said to me one day:

"Mr. Abe. I'm not being a sissy about this, am I?"

"No," I assured him. "This is a pretty serious injury."

"Well," he said, "if I ever am, you be sure to let me know."

That in a nutshell tells you all need to know about Steve Freeman.

Joe Cribbs

When he arrived as a rookie running back out of Auburn in 1980 he gave us the skill we needed to become a division champion and a playoff contender.

Joe was a talented and dedicated team player. He also fell as hard for the old Thanksgiving Turkey Hoax as any rookie we ever had.

The Bills, like some other teams, had a traditional prank they used to play on rookies at holiday time. The rookies were told that a local butcher, a huge fan and team supporter, was giving a free 20-pound turkey to each Bills player who showed up at his shop to claim one. All the player had to do was show up and identify himself to collect the bird.

Of course, the butcher had to play along with the hoax. It also required some courage when confronted by an angry 280-pound football player.

When the player asked for his bird, the butcher would say, "There is no free turkey. The turkey is you."

When word of the free turkey offer spread through the locker room on the day before Thanksgiving, Joe was one of the first to shower and dress and head for the butcher shop.

In Cribbs's rookie year we added a new twist to the plot. We sent Henry Kunttu, our team photographer, over to the butcher shop to secretly film what went on. Henry hid in the back room of the shop and filmed the rookies coming in for their turkey.

The next day at Thanksgiving Day practice, all the veteran players had fun razzing the rookies who had fallen for the turkey hoax. Cribbs, though, insisted he was not taken in and never showed up to collect his "free" bird.

The evidence was on film, of course, and we had Cribbs's visit spliced in with the game tape, which was shown at the team meeting and film review before practice that day. Cribbs was still denying that he was gullible to fall for the trick when the scene of him entering the shop flashed on the screen. There was Joe walking into the shop wearing his Auburn University lettermen's jacket with the big "AU" on it. You couldn't miss him. Then he started arguing with the butcher.

We all had a good laugh over it.

Frank Lewis

Frank came to us from the Pittsburgh Steelers in 1978 and he turned out to be a valuable acquisition. He was a real pro and had a good influence on our young receivers, especially Jerry Butler, our first-round pick in 1979.

In Butler's rookie season, he got some advice from Lewis that Jerry probably remembers to this day.

We had a third down and 22 on our own 30-yard line and Joe Ferguson threw a pass over the middle for a 5-yard gain. Butler caught the ball and got hammered by the defense and was knocked silly.

I went out to attend to him and help him to the bench. As Butler sat there gathering his senses, Lewis sauntered over and sat down next to him.

"Jerry," he said. "Don't always believe everything the coach tells you. You don't have to catch the ball at all costs. Just make sure they don't catch it. Just knock the ball down. Even if you catch it, it's still fourth-and-18 and we're going to punt without you getting KO'd."

Gary Marangi

Marangi was a young quarterback from Boston College who backed up Ferguson in the mid '70s. Gary didn't get much chance to play but he did get one opportunity in a late season game against the Minnesota Vikings in Orchard Park in 1975.

It was a cold day and there were snow banks on the sidelines and snow in the stands of the stadium. The Vikings handled us pretty easily that day with Chuck Foreman running wild. Foreman left the game finally after he was hit in the eye by a snowball thrown from the stands.

Late in the game Marangi came in to mop up at quarterback. With the clock winding down, he started using his timeouts and killing the clock with sideline patterns.

The Vikings were cold and angry and anxious to get out of there before anybody else got hurt.

The Purple People Eaters, as their defensive line of Jim Marshall, Alan Page, Carl Eller and Gary Larsen was known, began to get angry with Marangi.

"What are you doing calling time out, Rookie," they asked. They would have killed Marangi if they could have.

Marangi bravely walked over to them and said: "Hey, I never get the chance to play very much. This is my one chance. Please bear with me."

With that one of the Vikings said:

"Go ahead, kid. Knock yourself out. We like your spunk."

Bill Enyart

The year we drafted O.J., we also picked Enyart in the second round as a fullback to block for the Juice.

Enyart was a naïve guy from Oregon State. When he came to Buffalo to sign his contract, they took him sightseeing. Bob Lustig, the general manager at the time, asked Bill if there was anything in particular he would like to see. Niagara Falls, perhaps?

Enyart had one request. He wanted to see the Erie Canal and spent 10 minutes gazing at it.

J. D. Hill

Nobody had a higher threshold of pain than J.D.

We were playing a preseason game in Detroit. J.D. tore up his knee returning the second half kickoff.

When we got back to Buffalo we had the knee looked at.

"My back's killing me, too," J.D. told the doctor.

When they X-rayed his back they found that he had two broken transverse processes in his back. He told us that he hurt his back on the opening kickoff, which means he played the whole first half with the two broken bones, an injury that's as painful as having a couple of broken ribs.

Actually, J.D. was a good blocker for a receiver. His nickname was "Crack Back" Hill.

Once Lou Saban got mad at his wide receivers because he didn't think they were blocking enough for O.J. Finally, one week he ordered the full facemasks put on the helmets of the wide receivers in place of the double bars.

It lasted about a week, but the receivers got the message.

Joe DeLamielleure

One of the finest pass blockers we ever had, even though he was short and squat by present-day standards. His career with the Bills almost ended before it began. When he reported after the draft we gave him the usual physical, and an abnormality showed up in his EKG. We sent him to Emory University Hospital in Atlanta for a second opinion and he came back with a clean bill of health. The doctors were not concerned because he never had a prior history of any problems and he played all through high school and college at Michigan State with no problem.

Joe D was a gym rat. He would spend 7-8 hours a day in the training facility at the stadium working out. Most coaches would have admired that dedication, but Saban was bothered by it.

Whenever Saban came down to the trainers' room at lunchtime for our daily card game, Joe D always seemed to be there.

I related to Lou how dedicated Joe was.

"Next time he comes in, send him up to my office," Saban said.

I did and when they met, Saban asked Joe, "How long do you expect to play football?"

"Until I'm 35 or 40, coach," Joe replied.

"How long do you expect to live, Joe?" Lou said.

"I hope to be 75, at least, coach," Joe answered.

"What are you going to do between 35 and 75, Joe?" Lou asked.

Joe said, "I don't know."

"What did you take in school?" Lou asked.

"Criminal justice," Joe replied.

Lou then advised Joe that he could get the entire workout he needed in half the time. He should spend the rest of the day doing something to prepare him for life after football.

Joe ended up working at the Erie County Holding Center downtown to get a taste of what a career in criminal justice might be like.

He learned quickly that criminal justice was not where he really wanted to be. He went back to school and received a degree in education, which is one of the things he did after he stopped playing in the NFL.

DeLamielleure was a good athlete. He finished second in the NFL Players racquetball championship. Rafael Septien, the Dallas Cowboys' kicker, beat Joe in the tournament finals in Las Vegas one year.

I could beat a lot of our players in racquetball. As good as Joe was, I could even beat him once in a while – on a Monday. I always made sure

I played Joe on a Monday, when he was still stiff and sore from playing a Sunday football game.

You have to know when to pick your spots.

Once I was beating tight end Keith McKeller in racquetball. Ulysses Norris, another of our tight ends, was watching.

"If I can't beat that fat guy in racquetball, I won't play it ever again," Norris said, as he challenged me to a $5 game.

I beat him and I don't think he's played since.

Darryl Talley

Some say Talley was the heart and soul of our Super Bowl teams. His career didn't start off so well, however.

In his rookie year he was struggling on the field. He was a second-round draft pick out of West Virginia, but not playing like it.

One game in particular he was struggling and at halftime the defensive coaches were getting on him pretty good.

It turns out that we had Talley fitted out for contact lenses when he took his first physical after the draft.

When the coaches stopped yelling at him, I asked Darryl if he was wearing his contact lenses.

"No," he said.

"Well, put them in," I ordered.

Things got better for him right after that. He had a terrific second half that day and went on to a long and successful career as a Bill.

Jack Horrigan

Jack was the Bills' vice president of public relations when he died in 1973. He was a best friend – someone you could always turn to for good advice when you needed it. He was a very positive influence on O.J. during his years with the Bills. The Juice's ability to deal with the media was largely due to Jack's coaching.

It was a great loss to the Bills when he died. I really believe that some of the struggles the organization went through in the early 1970s would have been avoided if Jack had remained healthy. He was more than a good public relations man or press agent; he had a sense of right and wrong and had a good handle on the pulse of the organization. He knew what the players, coaches and staff were thinking, what the mood was, what was troubling them and what could be done to make things better. He was just a great person.

When he was being treated for cancer in his final months, Jack agreed to be a human guinea pig for some experimental anti-cancer drugs. He did it unselfishly.

Like my wife, Pat, Jack was proud of his Irish heritage. He used to insist that when Pat and I were married we should have taken her family name, Casey, instead of Abramoski.

He used to kid me about that all the time. That really was my only beef with Jack. After all, I'm just as proud of my Polish heritage as he was of his Irish roots.

Jack left behind a wonderful family. His son, Joe, is the Vice President of Communications at the Pro Football Hall of Fame in Canton.

CHAPTER 10

*"Close to being broke . . .
without really being broke."*

Mostly, this book is about the people and events I've dealt with in my years as the Bills' trainer. I would be remiss, though, without some words about the men I worked with on the medical staff and some of the situations we faced over the years.

Earlier, I mentioned Dr. James Sullivan, the first team doctor. After him came Dr. Joe Godfrey, then Dr. Richard Weiss and finally Dr. John Marzo. Dr. Godfrey started out as a general practitioner and then became an orthopedist. Dick Weiss was a mechanical engineer and a successful salesman before he decided to go to medical school. I think he was 40 when he became a doctor.

Once Dr. Godfrey was at Mercy Hospital finishing up a surgery when they brought to the emergency room a kid who had been in a bad accident. The surgeons were going to amputate the kid's leg. Dr. Godfrey intervened and performed the surgery that saved the young man's leg.

Years later, I had some business at a car dealership in Hamburg and was introduced to the lease manager.

"You won't remember me but ...." Then he proceeded to tell me how Dr. Godfrey had saved his leg.

The most serious injury of all my years with the Bills was the dislocated knee suffered by running back Roger Kochman in a game in Houston in 1962. We had some other bad knees — Bobby Burnett and Jerry Butler — but nothing like that, thank goodness.

Once in a game against the Titans at the Polo Grounds in New York, fullback Jack Spikes took a knee to the forehead and was knocked out.

Dr. Joseph Godfrey, whom I rate right with the best orthopedic surgeons in sports medicine, served the Bills from 1962 to 1978.

He swallowed his tongue. Dr. Godfrey and I had to force his jaw open and pull his tongue out so he could breathe. He suffered no ill effects.

Another scary injury came in a game in Houston in 1989. Cornerback Derrick Burroughs tried to tackle an Oilers receiver and got his head in an awkward position. When I got on the field, he wasn't breathing and I feared he had broken his neck. Just as we were about to turn him over and apply CPR he started breathing again. Carefully, we moved him to the X—ray room and saw that he did not have a broken neck. Further testing, however, showed that he had cervical stenosis, a narrowing of the canal through which the spinal cord runs. We recommended he not play again and he never did.

The closest we came to losing a player was in our first preseason, 1960. We had a big lineman from Minnesota named Ed Buckingham, who suffered a ruptured spleen during a preseason game. If we hadn't diagnosed him correctly and gotten him to a hospital, he might have bled to death. He was still in his uniform when they put him on the operating table.

When Korey Stringer, the 350-pound offensive tackle of the Minnesota Vikings, died of heat stroke in training camp in 2001, it made me realize how fortunate I had been in my 37 years as trainer with the Bills. When I heard the news about Stringer, I thought to myself, "Thank God something like that never happened to the Bills."

A lot of the credit for that goes to Dr. Godfrey and others. I think we were ahead of the curve as far as keeping players hydrated for games and practice.

Dr. Godfrey was involved in some World War II research with the military in getting infantrymen properly hydrated before long forced marches. In more recent times, Rusty Jones, our strength and conditioning coach, was instrumental in keeping us on the cutting edge.

We were one of the first teams to ad lib water breaks and allow the players to drink water any time they wanted to during practice. They didn't have to wait for the coach to call a water break. When we would play in a hot, humid place like Miami we would start preparing the players on the Monday before the game, getting them properly hydrated. We had plenty of water and fluids available and encouraged the players to drink as much as they could. We had signs and reminders posted all over the locker room.

It was never easy playing in the heat and humidity of Miami against good Dolphins teams, but I think we made the best of it and had our share of success down there because we were properly prepared for it.

It's not easy getting players to drink enough water. Some of them have a fear that they will have to urinate in the middle of a game.

One of the reasons we were able to get Frank Lewis, a wide receiver we obtained in a trade from Pittsburgh in 1978, was he had a history of hamstring problems. Once we got him, we made him drink a lot of water. The problem cleared up. Before we finally got him educated as to the amount of water one needed when playing in hot, humid environments, Frank would drink a glass of water and figure that was enough. It wasn't.

Our team dentist during nearly all of my years with the Bills was the late Dr. Steve Hudecki. He was another person who was truly a friend both professionally and personally. Once, before a big game with Miami, Robert James, our all-pro cornerback, came down with an ear ache. We had the doctor look at it. The doctor told Robert that the problem was not his ear but his tooth. Dr. Hudecki looked at the tooth and agreed that was the cause of the problem. Robert couldn't understand it when we wanted to send him to a dentist in Miami.

"Why do you guys want to mess around with my mouth when it's my ear that hurts?," he complained.

We got him to an oral surgeon anyway and almost as soon as the tooth was extracted the ear ache went away and Roberts finally was convinced that the tooth was the problem all the time. Sheepishly, he apologized to Dr. Hudecki for all the fuss he caused.

My first full-time assistant was Bob Reese. One reason I hired him was that he had also been trained at Purdue by Pinky Newell. So, we had been taught to do things the same way and both believed in Pinky's approach and philosophy. That cut down the time I needed to train him in the way I wanted things done. Besides that, he was a good guy.

When the New York Jets were looking for a trainer in the 1970s,

Johnny Mazur, one of their assistant coaches, called me to see if I was interested in the job. Mazur was an old Notre Dame quarterback who I had known since he was on Lou Saban's coaching staff in the 1960s.

Working in New York wasn't for me, but I recommended Bob Reese and he was hired.

His replacement was Bud Tice, who came to us from West Virginia University. He was another good trainer and a good guy with a sense of humor. When he left for an administrative job with Kaleida Health, we hired Bud Carpenter. "Carp" first helped us out during training camp at Fredonia State, where he worked as the athletics trainer and intramural director. He also helped us on game days in Orchard Park. "Carp" left Fredonia to be athletics trainer for the Boston Bruins of the National Hockey League. Then we brought him back to Western New York to replace Tice. He ended up succeeding me as head trainer when I retired.

I had a good relationship with all three guys and we've remained good friends to this day. One reason we worked so well together was that Bob and the two Buds were good at things I wasn't good at. I liked the nuts and bolts part of training, being on the field with the team and working with injured players. They were better organizers and better at handling the paper work and record keeping that comes with the job and keeps increasing every year because of insurance, legal and other concerns.

I had the same philosophy with all these guys. I wasn't the head trainer and they weren't the assistant trainer. We worked together; we did everything together. We did the same work. It wasn't "I do this because I'm the boss and you can only do that because you're not."

I trusted their work. Also, there was no rule that only I could work with the star players and they were left with the subs.

Bud Carpenter, in fact, worked very closely with Jim Kelly in his various injury rehabs and was a big reason Jim was able to come back and perform effectively after injuries — especially in the postseason during two of our Super Bowl years, 1990 and 1992.

Jim was comfortable working with Bud because they were friends. They played golf together and Jim seemed to have a lot of confidence in Bud's work. So it worked out best that way and it was no problem with me.

The Bills were fortunate to hire Rusty Jones as strength and conditioning coach in the mid 1980s and he played a major role in any success we had. Rusty is an exercise physiologist and very computer savvy. He helped set up a lot of the computer programs we used in training and quantifying the progress players were making in rehabilitation from injuries. He had a few misses, but his influence changed the dietary habits of a lot of our players. Some players had a dramatic decrease in body fat that made them more productive on the field.

Rusty and I saw eye-to-eye on a lot of things dealing with conditioning and nutrition. He had the knowledge and training to put a lot of things into practice.

In the 1990s our training staff expanded and we were able to add some very capable trainers to our full-time and part-time staff as well as some training camp interns of great promise in the profession.

Bill Ford was one good young trainer we were fortunate to have. The Bills ended up hiring one of those good summer interns — Greg McMillen, and we were fortunate to get him, too. Dean Eberle, one of our other interns, was the best taper we ever had and also the fastest.

A lot of people don't realize there is a difference between being a physical therapist and a trainer. A physical therapist can't be a trainer unless he knows how to tape. A trainer has to tape all the guys before a game or practice. You can't take seven minutes to tape each guy or you won't get the players on the field in time.

The hardest thing for a trainer is dealing with a player who is not intelligent and is afraid. You tell him you're going to have to do something and he doesn't want to do it because it might hurt. That's the hardest guy to get well. If a guy is very bright and you can explain things to him, usually he can follow the rehab routine, do it correctly and not get discouraged when the results are not immediate.

One thing I've learned: A pro football player will never do anything that doesn't benefit him. As soon as a player finds out something doesn't benefit him, he won't do it.

In my estimation, Dr. Joe Godfrey ranked right up there with the top sports doctors of his time — Jack Hughston, Marcus Stewart, Jim Nicholas, Donald O'Donohue, Bob Kerlan and Frank Jobe.

Those were the guys whose work in the field convinced the orthopedics community to recognize sports medicine as a field.

My biggest disappointments as a trainer came when players did not have enough confidence in our medical staff, but I could understand that. The guys, the doctors and trainers and specialists we referred injured players to, were as good as anybody there ever was and you could match their rate of success with anybody else's. But the grass always looks greener on the other side of the street.

The players, who are entitled to an outside opinion, think like this:

If this specialist in Colorado or Alabama is good enough for Jerry Rice, I should be going to him, too. That's the attitude some of them have.

As a trainer I got a great deal of self-satisfaction in being able to help a player get back on the field sooner than expected. I like to think the things we did hastened a player's recovery from an injury. Again, the most important thing I learned is that you have to treat every guy as an individual. You have to know what makes each individual tick. I used to consider myself a pseudo-psychiatrist. You have to know what buttons to push to get a player to overcome an injury.

And it took me five years to realize that when a guy says something hurts him, you have to accept that. Pain that keeps one guy out won't keep another out. You have to accept that. It was something that used to bother me but once I learned that lesson I was a much better trainer.

Of course, you have some players who were not hurt as badly as they thought.

In the 1970s we had a defensive end named Louis Ross. He hurt his hand in a game. I diagnosed it as a bad bruise, but Louis insisted it was broken.

"Eddie, I know this is broke," he kept telling me.

Finally after listening to this for a few days, I said, "OK, Louis, I talked to Dr. Godfrey and he said it was OK for you to have it X-rayed, but I'll bet you five bucks that thing isn't broken."

"Oh, no. It sure is," he insisted.

A few hours later he came back from the X-ray.

"Well, Louis is it broken?" I asked.

"Eddie, you won't believe this," he said. "That X-ray technician said this hand was as close to being broke as it could be without really being broke. So, do I have to pay you the five dollars?"

Needless to say, I never collected on that bet.

We had another defensive end in the '80s named Scott Virkus.

In one game he was down on the field after a play and I went out to see what was wrong. He started giving me all this complex stuff about what hurt him — a lot of self-diagnosis.

I said, "Hey, you're no Phi Beta Kappa. Just tell me where you hurt."

"Right, I'm not a Phi Beta Kappa," he said. "I'm a Lambda Chi Alpha."

The Pinky Newell philosophy of treating every guy the same has given me some nice rewards.

In the past year, I got two phone calls from a kid named Herve Dumas. He was a linebacker from Hofstra, a free agent, who was injured in training camp a few years ago. Even though he was a fringe player, I worked hard with him on the rehabilitation of his knee. He told me he appreciated all the attention I showed him even though he wasn't a top player. Now he's running a wellness clinic in New Jersey. He said the way I worked with him inspired him to want to get into the training profession.

Over the years I helped a lot of local high school athletes. Coaches would bring kids to our training room for treatment. Once I got a little static about it for providing the free treatments, but Dr. Godfrey backed me up all the way. On Mondays or Tuesdays, when the Bills had their normal day off, there might be a dozen local high school athletes in our training room for injury treatment because the coaches knew we could get them back on the field faster than if they went through their normal channels.

I also worked rehabbing injuries with professional athletes in other sports. Dr. Weiss was an orthopedics consultant for the Boston Bruins and often sent players to me. Bruins such as Gord Kluzak, Brad Park and

Wayne Cashman made special trips to Buffalo to start rehabilitation under me after knee surgery.

I also rehabbed NBA center Bob Lanier after he had his first knee surgery when he was injured playing for St. Bonaventure in the 1970 NCAA tournament.

Of all the friendships I made in my years with the Bills, the ones I value most are the ones with the trainers and doctors I worked beside all those years.

When I started out, I was more than a trainer to Bills players, especially the rookies. I had to teach them a lot of things to help them deal with ordinary day-to-day life. I started checking accounts for some. I taught them how to buy a car or a house. I set up the financing. There were a lot of little things they would come to me for.

I really felt rewarded and I enjoyed every minute of it. I enjoyed it so much I would show up for work earlier than I had to. Except for the time when I had my own knee surgery, I never missed work. During one training camp I was allowed to go home at night to sleep. That was the year Pat and I flipped over our van on the New York Thruway coming back from Erie. Pat suffered a broken bone in her neck so I went home every night for a couple of weeks to help her out.

Even though it wasn't glamorous work, I never thought about getting another job except during the mid 1980s, after a couple of those 2-14 seasons. I was a little discouraged by all the losing.

One day I came home and said to Pat, "We're never going anywhere." It seemed every time we'd go to the trainers' convention somebody would be getting a ring or an award and talking about this bowl team or that playoff team or this championship team.

I'm the eternal optimist but when something goes wrong, I really get down. Pat is sort of a balance between the two and gets me back on an even keel.

Pat wouldn't let me quit the Bills.

"Hey," she said. "How would you like to be one of those guys who is out of a job at Bethlehem Steel? The team is not winning many games, but you're getting a good paycheck. You've got five good daughters at home and everything else is fine."

After that talk, it seemed our fortunes with the Bills began to change.

Sometimes the medical side thinks it knows football, too, and vice versa.

I remember once in a game against the New York Jets one of their linemen, Roger Finnie, suffered a broken ankle near our sideline.

I got to him first. Dr. James Nicholas, the Jets team physician, and coach Weeb Ewbank came on the field with Jeff Snedeker, the Jets' trainer.

A fourth-and-one situation was facing the Jets. Now, as we were all leaning over the fallen Phinnie, Dr. Nicholas was telling Weeb to go for it on fourth down. Weeb was telling Dr. Nicholas that Phinnie's ankle isn't broken.

Snedeker turned to me and said:

"Eddie, what am I going to do? I've got a doctor who thinks he's a coach and a coach who thinks he's a doctor."

Left is Bud Carpenter, with Abe, Bud Tice and Bob Reese.

CHAPTER 11

The Super Years

Things began to turn around for the Bills when the USFL folded in 1986 and we signed quarterback Jim Kelly.

We already had Bruce Smith, Andre Reed, Darryl Talley and Will Wolford and picked up center Kent Hull and linebacker Ray Bentley when the USFL folded, but we were lacking an established quarterback after Joe Ferguson was traded away.

We were down in Houston for a preseason game when they negotiated the contract with Kelly. I was taping when Bill Polian brought him into the training room before the game. I was pleased we had finally gotten a quarterback who was going to do something. I had a good gut feeling right from the start about him and it turned out to be right. It started a terrific run for us when we got him.

I don't know what we paid him but he was worth every penny that he got. The players realized, too, that they finally had a chance to win because they got somebody who can pass the ball.

I was as pleased as anybody when Jim was elected to the Pro Football Hall of Fame the first time he became eligible for induction.

Building the Super Bowl Bills didn't happen overnight. Halfway through the 1986 season, Marv Levy took over as head coach and that was a big thing. And in the next couple of drafts we added players like Thurman Thomas, Shane Conlan, Nate Odomes and Howard Ballard and acquired veterans like Steve Tasker, James Lofton, Leonard Smith, John Davis and Kenneth Davis and traded for the rights to Cornelius Bennett.

Marv Levy and Steve Tasker -- two "special" people who were instrumental in much of our success in the 1990s.

The Bills claimed Tasker when the Houston Oilers tried to sneak him through waivers and activate him during the 1986 season. We brought Tasker in for his physical. The Oilers had instructed him to tell us that his knee was killing him so the Bills would fail him and he could go back to Houston. Dr. Weiss, in fact, was going to fail him but Bill Polian, our general manager, asked that he be passed because we really needed him. Dr. Weiss did pass him, but noted that Tasker would need surgery down the line.

A couple of years later, Dr. Weiss did perform surgery on Tasker's knee and Steve went on to the fabulous career he enjoyed as our special teams ace and extra receiver.

The Bills' breakthrough began in 1988 when we got to the AFC championship game. We started 4-0 without Bruce Smith, who had been suspended by the league. We played the Bears in Chicago his first game back and we got blown out. We played a horrible game. We had a lot of injuries at Chicago. I always hated to play there, because every time we played in Chicago we got dinged up.

The 1989 season is known as the year of the Bickering Bills. We lost at Cleveland in the second round of the playoffs, the only time in a six-year stretch that we didn't get to the AFC championship game.

I thought that Bickering Bills stuff was overblown. You could say the players bickered but it was like squabbling among brothers. Once it was over, it was over. They were buddies and were able to work together. If anybody tried to take advantage of one of us, the guys would rally around each other like family.

Finally, in 1990 we broke through and got to the Super Bowl.

It was a magical season. It was amazing to watch us score 21 points in a span of 77 seconds against Denver. A game we were losing turned completely around. Then the next week we came from behind and beat the Raiders.

By the end of the season we were using the no-huddle as our primary offense. We had opened the season with it when we beat Indianapolis at home, but didn't use it much until early December, when it blew out Buddy Ryan's Philadelphia Eagles, a very good team.

In the AFC championship game we beat the Raiders, 51-3. I really wasn't surprised that we handled them so easily. I knew that Oakland wasn't a well-conditioned football team. If you remember our first drive of the game they had to call time out twice. They couldn't keep pace with our no-huddle offense. During the timeouts, they were all sitting on their helmets. Their big guys were beat. We scored a touchdown in a minute and 20 seconds the first time we got the ball.

Before they actually experienced it, the Raiders had no clue as to how fast the pace of the game was going to be. I know people look at game film and stuff, but you're not seeing the game in real time. The camera gets shut off between plays.

I think they were run ragged. I think they ran out of gas. From talking to the late Bobby Chandler, an old Bill who finished his career with the Raiders, I knew how they did things in the past.

The Raiders had to work twice as hard because they were going at a pace double what they were used to. The big guys didn't have time to recover.

Another amazing game was the comeback against Houston in the wild-card round of the 1992 playoffs. We were behind 28-3 at the half and it was 35-3 early in the third quarter, but we came back to win, 41-38, on Steve Christie's field goal in overtime.

Frank Reich was the quarterback because Jim Kelly was out with a knee injury. Reich threw four touchdown passes to Andre Reed in the second half to lead the greatest comeback in NFL history.

Funny thing, I thought at halftime we had a chance to come back even though it was 28-3.

Coming out of the tunnel for the second half, I said to Dr. Weiss, "We got the ball first. If we score it's 28-10 and we got a chance to be in the game."

We went on the field and Frank Reich threw that interception that made it 35-3. I told Doc, "I hope we don't get embarrassed like the day we beat Oakland."

I can remember Darryl Talley coming off the field after they scored and telling the guys,

"Hey, we got them right where we want them now." He was yelling.

I thought he was crazy. I told Doc Weiss, there was no way we can come back in this game. "We're done for," I said.

But little by little, Houston started to play not to lose and they didn't play to win. They went into like a shell and Frank — this shows you what a guy with a sound football mind can accomplish –- began to attack them. He didn't have the greatest arm but he had terrific knowledge of the game. He was one of the big reasons why Kelly was such a good player here, too. Jim didn't feel threatened by Frank. He listened to Frank a lot in their everyday dealings and talked about the game and they had a mutual respect. Frank knew his role, too. I think if he decided to, he would be a terrific coach.

The coaches made some major adjustments at halftime, too. Walt Corey, our defensive coordinator, had put in all this fancy stuff to stop Houston's run-and-shoot offense. We started the game with extra backs on the field to match up with their wide receivers. When the score was 28-3 at halftime, Walt put us back in base defense and our linebackers were forced to cover their receivers and backs. We won the game playing basic defense, no frills, and no nothing.

When those little Houston receivers came across the middle, the linebackers, Cornelius Bennett and Darryl Talley, would smack them and they weren't too keen on catching the ball after that. When we had all those defensive backs in the game, they went up and down the field like we weren't even there.

It's like we always used to say. "The prevent defense — the only thing it prevents is us winning."

*Frank Reich and Pete Metzelaars -- two of our underrated guys
who exemplified the great character of the 90s teams.*

CHAPTER 12

The Super Bills

One thing the Super Bowl Bills of the 1990s had in common with the Buffalo AFL championship teams of the '60s was that both had a lot of bright guys — Steve Tasker, Bruce Smith, Kent Hull, John Davis, Will Wolford, Thurman Thomas, Andre Reed, Darryl Talley, Jim Kelly, James Lofton, Pete Metzelaars, Howard Ballard, Phil Hansen, Ray Bentley, Cornelius Bennett, Nate Odomes, Mark Kelso, Don Beebe, Glenn Parker, Marvcus Patton, Jim Ritcher, Henry Jones. Maybe they all weren't intellectuals but they were all smart and most of them had personality.

Not only were they smart, they were street smart.

The glue of those '90s teams was Talley. He was a guy who was not afraid to confront a Bruce Smith or a Cornelius Bennett or a Jim Kelly.

Over a four-year period we had 17 different guys go to the Pro Bowl. That's a pretty good indication of how good they were and Marv Levy did a terrific job to keep all that talent together.

Of course, some of them weren't as smart as they'd like you to think.

Take Bruce Smith, for example. After he had been around for a while, he began to think he was pretty articulate — the great orator. You could see it when the media was interviewing him. During one interview, however, he misspoke — kind of got his metaphors mixed.

"That's water under the dam," (sic) he said.

Naturally, his teammates picked it up and never let him forget it.

Whenever the guys got into deep discussions about football and things in general, Bruce liked to think his opinion was always right, always

Thurman Thomas celebrates with is offensive line for a job well done.

superior, always so well-thought out. He was another World-ologist, like Fred Smerlas. Guys like Odomes, Talley, Kelly and Thurman knew how to shut Bruce up.

"That's water under the dam. Right, Bruce?"

Once, when we were playing Cincinnati, Bruce got into a collision with a 178-pound wide receiver. Bruce went down like he was shot. He caught an elbow in the thigh and he was on the ground moaning and holding his leg. Meanwhile, the 178-pound guy popped up after the collision and trotted off the field as if nothing had happened.

We went out to attend to Bruce, who was still down. Darryl Talley came over and asked me what happened.

I said, "he got elbowed in the thigh."

Talley said to Bruce, "You mean to tell me that little 178-pound bastard elbowed you in the thigh and you can't get up. Get your ass up. Let's go."

And Bruce played.

There was always a lot of bantering back and forth in the training room between the players and myself and among the players. If you slipped up just once, somebody would always remember it and it would come back to haunt you.

Even Tasker had his moments. One year he received a plaque from a school group for his sportsmanship.

The great sportsman. Two days before, he got upset over a call in the game and really started getting on one of the officials.

"Hey," he said to the zebra. "There are 22 guys (the players) out here doing a professional job and not one of them is wearing stripes."

During training camp when things quieted down at night, I used to play hearts in the trainers' room with Bud Carpenter, Tasker, John Kidd. Pete Metzelaars, Frank Reich and Gale Gilbert. We'd usually order a pizza and chicken wings and have them delivered.

One night, a kid delivered the pizza and wings. The bill came to something like $13.50 and John Kidd pulled out a 20-dollar bill to pay for the food and handed it to Tasker to pass to the delivery guy.

"Here, keep the change," Tasker told the delivery guy. "We pride ourselves on being big tippers around here."

Big tipper? The night before when it was Tasker's turn to pay for the food, he tipped the kid just the loose change. We never let him forget that.

Off course, I got caught a few times, too.

Once I was taping Jim Kelly's knee before practice. He had propped himself up on the trainer's table while we were talking and I just started taping — the wrong knee.

"The great trainer doesn't even know which knee to tape. I'm glad you're not operating on me," Kelly would say.

Kelly was one of the toughest guys I've ever dealt with. Whenever you'd count him out with an injury, he'd always prove you wrong and be back there. He got knocked out a few times and went back in the game. Twice he came back from knee injuries to take us to the Super Bowl. He recovered in time to lead us over Miami and the Raiders before Super Bowl XXV. And in 1993, after Frank Reich had quarterbacked us to wins over Houston and Pittsburgh, Jim came back for the win at Miami in the AFC championship game.

The biggest thing about Kelly was how gracious and giving he was. He was a tough guy who loved his mother and father and family. He always took as good care of them as he could. His mom eventually died of emphysema. Because of her condition it was difficult for her to travel from their home in East Brady, Pa., to Buffalo for games. Jim bought them a motor home so they could drive up to the games in comfort. He took care of his five brothers, too. He always bought them beautiful Christmas gifts. And he did a lot of things for a lot of people.

The same thing with the training staff and equipment guys. He always took good care of us. He was a real genuine guy.

One thing that helped bring the Super Bowl Bills together was the team parties Kelly used to have after home games at the big house he had built in Orchard Park. The place was awesome, especially the game room with all the memorabilia he had collected from his friends in sports.

I went there once to see it all because I had heard so much about it, but I made it a point not to go to the team parties. If something happened at one of the parties, I didn't want to be there. If somebody — the coach or general manager — asked me about it, I could honestly say, "I don't know." If you hang around with the players you put yourself in jeopardy. If the head coach or somebody else asks you what happened over there, you have to either lie or put the guy on the spot.

I don't think a trainer should socialize with the guys. They were my friends but I had to draw a line. I'd play cards with them on the plane and at night at training camp. I'd love that stuff but I never went to many team gatherings after games. For years it's been a tradition for a lot of the players to go to Ilio DiPaolo's restaurant with their wives after games. Ilio, before he died, and his sons, Dennis and Michael, would have a private room ready for them so they could relax, have a few beers and eat some good Italian food. I only went two or three times over the years. I always used the excuse that I had to go home and feed my pigeons.

When I was younger I did more things with the guys, because I was more their age. Also, we had fewer players so we were a lot closer. For example, when we'd go to a place like Denver in the AFL years, there might be a group of 15 or 20 players eating out together. They had a restaurant there called Joe's Awful Coffee. An ex-fighter owned it. We'd always go there with a big group of players. The camaraderie carried over onto the field.

Pete Metzelaars, the tight end on our Super Bowl teams, was another good guy. He never showed up in the morning without a little something — coffee and donuts or cookies for the training staff. Pete and I used to have a lot of good discussions about everything under the sun.

Pete had gone to Wabash, a little college in Indiana where he was a big basketball star as well as a football player.

When he needed to be put in his place, I'd say something like:

"Is that the way they do it at Wabash?"

Then, I'd sing the "Wabash Cannonball" song for him.

I'm not much of a singer, but I do know parts of a lot of songs. Dave Hojnowski, the Bills' equipment manager, always said that I know the first line of more songs than anybody else in the world. The first line, that's all.

Running back Thurman Thomas is still one of my best friends. When I retired he used to call me every day when he was here. As soon as he came back to town for spring minicamp he would give me a call.

Of course, we used to trade insults every day. He'd call me a fat so-and-so and I would call him "short ass."

"I could eat pie off your head," I'd say to him.

"You're so fat you can't tie your shoes. You haven't seen your (genitals) in years," he would answer back.

We'd go back and forth like that, but we were really good friends. That's why I made it a point to show up at his retirement announcement. It was out of respect for him. He was a guy who always played to win. He's not a guy who would ever take a day off. Over the years, we had guys with more talent but not his desire.

One of the biggest wastes of talent we ever had was Greg Bell, a running back out of Notre Dame in the '80s. Ahmad Rashad was probably the best pure athlete the Bills ever had. He could excel in any sport — tennis, basketball, baseball.

Bell was a great athlete, too. He ran the 60-yard dash in the Millrose Games in New York as a high school track guy and played on a two-time state basketball champion in Columbus, Ohio, and was a great football player. His problem was — although he probably wouldn't admit it — he really didn't like football that much. At least not enough to be a full-time professional. It's a tough game when you don't like something.

Some players had athletic talent but lacked what Marv Levy used to call football temperament. I call it durability and availability. Pro football is availability. Anybody can play this game when they're 100 percent but if you aren't durable and ready to play, you can have all the talent in the world. Durability is a big, big plus.

Judging who has what it takes to play pro football is a tricky business. The 1987 college draft was a good example of that. We were looking for a linebacker with the eighth pick and the choice seemed to be between Mike Junkin of Duke and Shane Conlan of Penn State.

Junkin tested out as the superior athlete at the combine in Indianapolis. The scouts loved his combination of size and speed. There was one problem though: Don't you think that Mike Junkin at Duke, being the biggest, strongest and fastest, would be able to dominate the game? He should be making tackles all over the place, like Zach Thomas does for Miami now. Junkin didn't even lead Duke in tackles.

Conlan, on the other hand, didn't test as well at the combine, and below the waist didn't look like much of a football player with those thin legs. But he was always making the big interception or the big stop for Penn State. Remember the Fiesta Bowl game against Miami, when he intercepted Vinny Testaverde to wrap up the game?

As it turned out Cleveland drafted Junkin just before our turn came. I was glad because I guarantee you we would have taken Junkin. Instead, we got left with Conlan, who turned out to be the better player.

One reason we were able to draft a back as good as Thurman Thomas in the second round in 1988 was we did our homework. Thurman had suffered a serious knee injury in his sophomore year and that scared the rest of the league away. He had never had surgery on it.

We did a lot of research on Thurman. I knew the trainer at Oklahoma State, Jeff Fair, and he told me that knee had been no problem to Thurman his last two years. He never missed a game or practice and hardly ever visited the training room.

Even though Thurman had a damaged ligament and cartilage he had bony stability in the knee. The joint just meshed together well. It was something he was born with. Some athletes have just the opposite.

Still, we would not have taken Thurman as early as we did if Ralph Wilson wasn't willing to take a chance on a player with a knee history.

I was in the draft room when we selected Thurman. I remember Mr. Wilson saying, "The whole draft is a crapshoot anyway, so we might as well roll the dice."

As it turned out Thurman never had any problems with the knee. He missed a few games during his career in Buffalo because of other injuries, but the knee held up for 12 seasons. Ironically, his career ended with the Miami Dolphins when he tore the ACL on the other knee.

Howard "House" Ballard, the right offensive tackle on our Super Bowl teams, was an enormous guy with an enormous appetite.

We were a happy bunch as we left the Los Angeles Coliseum in 1991 after beating the Raiders in overtime on Scott Norwood's field goal. I was on the last bus to leave the Coliseum for the trip to the L.A. Airport and the charter plane back to Buffalo.

"House," who was 6-feet-6 and weighed 330 pounds, hadn't eaten since the morning pregame meal and he was getting mighty hungry. When the bus passed by a Church's Chicken place in South Central L.A., Howard told the driver, "Bussie, stop here for a few minutes. I want to run in and get some food."

The bus driver said, "I can't." We were in a hurry to get to the airport and a police escort was leading us. But Ballard insisted and the driver finally gave in.

Ballard went in and bought everything they had on the racks — all the chicken, French fries, rolls, bread — everything. He spent about $300. We all started eating fried chicken, even the bus driver. I can still picture him driving the bus with one hand, and gnawing on a drumstick with the other.

Of course, when we get to the plane, Bill Polian, the general manager, is waiting there on the tarmac and he is steaming.

"Where were you guys?" he said.

"Here, have some chicken, Mr. Polian," House said.

Joe Devlin missed our Super Bowl run, unfortunately, after a long career with the Bills. He was a very intense player and a very reliable performer on the offensive line through a lot of years.

He was playing right guard for us in a game at Houston in 1989 and early in the game one of the Oilers went through Devlin and sacked Kelly. It ruined a drive we had going.

When the offense came off the field, Tom Bresnahan, who was the new offensive line coach at the time, went over to Devlin and asked what happened.

"It was my fault," Devlin said. "The guy just jumped the snap. I wasn't ready for it. It's my fault. I won't let it happen again."

Devlin went over and sat down on the bench to rest. Here comes Bresnahan back to press the issue. "God dang it, Joe, what happened out there?" he asked again.

"I told you," Joe said. "He jumped the count, coach. Sorry. It won't happen again. That's it."

Bresnahan walked away, but a few seconds later he came back.

By this time Devlin was fuming.

Joe said, "If you come back one more time, I'm going to grab you by the freaking neck and throttle you."

Center Kent Hull was sitting there taking it all in as he sipped on his Gatorade. Hull calmly looked up at Bresnahan and said:

"He means it, Tom."

Bresnahan walked away and didn't mention it again.

Devlin was a different guy. More than 10 years later, he's still mad that the Bills cut him after the 1989 season. He took the game seriously and he trained hard and had great discipline.

In Chuck Knox's first year as coach, he came down to the training room one day in the offseason and asked, "Where's Joe Devlin. I've been around here for two weeks and I ain't seen him yet and I can't reach him on the phone."

"Neither can anybody else," I told him.

Knox was concerned because Devlin was coming back from surgery for a broken ankle he suffered the season before.

"Don't worry, Coach," I said. "He'll be at minicamp."

Anyway, Devlin came back in perfect shape, no trouble with the ankle.

I asked him how he did it.

He said that when he got the strength back in the leg, he put on his combat boots and ran in the woods every day until everything loosened up and the soreness went away. End of story.

Of course, we lost the four Super Bowls in a row but still there's a lot to be thankful for.

The first time I was just thankful to get there. I never thought it would happen in my career. When we beat Oakland for the AFC championship, Cornelius Bennett, Darryl Talley, Pete Metzelaars, Kent Hull, Thurman Thomas and Jim Kelly came up to me in the locker room after we came off the field.

"We're going to the big show, Eddie," they said.

I got all choked up and started crying real tears.

Losing the first one to the New York Giants, 20-19, bothered me the most because I thought we had the best chance to win that one. Until then, I had never been to a Super Bowl, so the game in Tampa was the most memorable to me.

I had always told myself I would never go to a Super Bowl unless we won the right to go. It was my first opportunity to see all the things that go along with the Super Bowl. Until I saw it first hand, I never realized how big it was.

Super Bowl XXV was during Desert Storm. I remember Whitney Houston singing the national anthem and the jets flying over. When Bruce Smith tackled Giants quarterback Jeff Hostetler for a safety, I thought "We're on our way, man." It didn't turn out that way. We lost when Scott Norwood's field goal went wide right with three seconds to go.

I've always felt sorry for Norwood. It shouldn't have come down to that because I thought we were a better football team than they were. We would have been thought of as a dynasty had we won one of those games.

The other game that hurt was when we were playing Dallas in Atlanta and we were winning at halftime. Then Pete Metzelears and Phil Hansen got hurt and the Cowboys took over the game in the second half. The Washington game in Minneapolis and the other Dallas game in Pasadena, we were just out of.

Mr. Wilson really took care of the help in the Super Bowl years. With the exception of one year, I got what amounted to a player's full share of Super Bowl money. To me that was big-time money. One of the first things I did was build a new loft for my racing pigeons. The one I had was 32-33 years old. Since I knew I would soon be retiring, I knew I could use a new modern loft. So we took about $10,000 and had one built. I built it so that it would be easier for me to take care of and clean. I made my own plan. I went to Belgium, where pigeon racing is the national sport, and saw how their lofts were built. They're fully automated. They even have conveyor belts to collect the droppings and deposit them into a basket.

Pigeon racing was a hobby I learned from my uncle, Teddy, back in Erie. I call it the Poor Man's Thoroughbred Racing and it's something that I really enjoy doing in my retirement.

You might be surprised at how I've been able to connect with people in football because of a mutual interest in pigeon racing. Terry Bradshaw, Merlin Olsen and Joe Hergert, a Bills linebacker in the early 1960s, are players who are into pigeon racing. Freddie Benners, a quarterback at SMU and later the New York Giants, is another old NFL player who was into the sport. There are other celebrities, who I have not met but have read about, who are into the sport. Singer Ray Price and the Italian designer Gucci are some others. Gucci once read about a championship bird in Buffalo and had his agent call and purchase the bird.

One of the rewards for being a trainer at the Super Bowl was getting invited to the Indianapolis 500 as guests of Stokley-Van Camp's, the company that made Gatorade. Pat and I watched the race from a special box right on the first turn. Fantastic.

Another benefit of going to the Super Bowl was that my whole family was able to go: my five daughters and their husbands. They all got to see Tampa, Minneapolis, Los Angeles and Atlanta. Again, that was due to the generosity of Mr. Wilson, who chartered a plan to take the families of the players and staff to the games.

The Super Bowl routine wasn't much different than a regular season game. They all seem to blend together now. In Super Bowl XXVI we were assigned to the University of Minnesota. I liked that because Tim Kirschner, the assistant trainer there, had been an assistant with Eddie Block with the Baltimore Colts, so I knew him. He was also a pigeon flier.

When Kirschner was with the Colts, he and I used to talk on the field before games during the warm-ups. People probably thought we were talking football or injuries but we usually were talking pigeon racing.

One thing the Super Bowls did was give me the financial security to allow me to retire and enjoy life. The bonus for going to the Super Bowl added to my salary and increased my pension so I could retire.

I had missed a lot during all those years I was a trainer. I was never able to go to my high school reunions or to any pigeon conventions and I missed the majority of the birthday parties for my five daughters and my friends' weddings because they were always in the summer months, when I was at training camp. But that was part of the price I paid for a rewarding career.

Abe (back Row, in center) with his five daughters and 13 grandchildren.

CHAPTER 13

Retirement:
Time for family and my pigeons

After all those seven-day weeks and 12-hour working days when I was the Bills trainer you would think I might have difficulty finding ways to fill my time. Nothing could be further from the truth.

First of all, I stay close to the Bills. I sit in the press box for all the home games and eat all that free food they give the media. I didn't know what I was missing all those years when I was freezing on the sidelines. The only thing I don't like about it is a rule they have: No cheering in the press box.

Seriously, though, it keeps me close to the team and the people in the organization. I always go down to the training room for a visit before and after the game, but I'm careful not to get in the way. It's their baby now.

I also attend a lot of Bills' functions - retirement ceremonies and such. A few times I've represented the team. In the spring of 2002 I went to Fort Sill in Lawton, Okla., where they were dedicating a recreation building on the base in the memory of Bob Kalsu, the Bills guard who was killed in the Vietnam War.

If I were still working, I probably would have missed the Hall of Fame inductions of Billy Shaw and Marv Levy in Canton, Ohio, and I will be proud to be there for Jim Kelly's induction in 2002.

Most of my traveling, though, is to visit my family, which is spread out across the Eastern U.S. One daughter, Cindy, lives in Ashburn, Va., where the Washington Redskins train. I think I'm slowly converting her husband, Paul, into a Buffalo fan. He's a staunch Redskins fan.

Pigeon racing and breeding has been my hobby for most of my life.

Pat and I also go to Reading, Pa., to visit another daughter, Jenny, who has two children. Now I can go to their First Communions, birthdays and graduations and things like that.

We also get to Green, Ohio, near Canton, to visit Carrie, the mother of Shawn, our adopted grandson. I also get to see Ellie and Nick, their other kids, at important times in their lives.

Closer to home, there is more time now to visit with our oldest daughter, Sophie, and her three children and the youngest of our daughters, Becky, and her son and daughter.

After missing so many high school reunions in Erie, Pa., I got to go back for my 50th reunion in 2001. I saw classmates I hadn't seen since graduating.

Aside from family and the Bills, most of my other free time is taken up by my hobby, pigeon racing.

As I mentioned before it was a sport I learned from my Uncle Teddy and it's provided me with many hours of fun and relaxation throughout my life.

It was good therapy to have a hobby like that when I needed to get away from football. When I needed to recharge my batteries, it was good to go off to the loft and sit and try to figure which birds I would send to the next race or how I would pair them in the next mating season to produce better birds.

Breeding pigeons is similar to breeding thoroughbred horses. For example, you try to mate a bird with more stamina with another bird with speed.

I've been a member of the Buffalo Homing Pigeon Association since 1962. These fliers are all top-notch pigeon people and you have to be on your toes if you expect to win against that competition.

Over the years, I've won some races in our club, but, of course, you're always trying to do better. I mentioned before the new loft I had built with the money I saved from our Super Bowls. That's helped me run a more efficient loft and easier to take care of. Also, I have more time to keep up with what's going on in the sport. I was able to attend the last two national pigeon conventions and got to meet a lot of terrific people and trade ideas and knowledge. Those conventions normally are held in the fall, right in the middle of the football season. When I was in football, I never was able to attend.

I've gained a little notoriety for my success in pigeon racing.

One year I had some birds entered in a race that was ending on the day we were playing a preseason game in Kansas City. That meant Pat would have to clock the birds when they returned to the loft after a 300-mile race.

I didn't expect to find out how my birds did until I got home in the wee hours of the morning after we flew back to Buffalo, but I got a pleasant surprise.

During the game, the phone rang on the sidelines. Usually it's somebody from the media relations staff asking the status of an injured player.

When the phone rang, one of the equipment boys picked it up and said, "Eddie, the phone's for you."

On the other end, I heard the voice of Paul Maguire, who was doing the color broadcast on TV with Rick Azar.

"Eddie," he said. "You won the 300."

"What are you talking about," I said.

"The pigeon race. You won the 300-mile pigeon race," he said.

It turns out that Pat had called the TV booth and given them the news. She was pretty excited about it, especially because we hadn't been having much success that year.

To be honest, I can't remember if the Bills won the game or not, but I know I won.

It's very common for the network television commentators to come to town a day or two before a Sunday game to prepare for the telecast. Besides studying the plays and defenses, they are looking for items of interest about the players - hobbies, interests and personal vignettes. When Merlin Olsen was with NBC he used to visit the trainers' room looking for background information he could use on the air. I usually cooperated. I like Merlin, who was a good guy. Also, he was a pigeon fancier. He had birds when he was a kid growing up in Utah.

One day, he came in and said:

"Eddie, for all the times you've helped me, we're going to talk about you today."

He spent about a minute and a half interviewing me about pigeon racing and what race was going on that weekend and other things about the sport.

Our public relations guy was standing by watching it all. He was impressed.

"You know what, Eddie," he said. "At the going rate for commercials on television these days, you just got about $150,000 of free advertising for your sport."

I've been asked a thousand times how a pigeon race is run. It's simple.

First of all, we select race stations from 100 to 600 miles. A race can be 100, 200 or 300 miles and so on.

We know the longitude and latitude at the release point and the longitude and latitude at the home left. This gives each individual competitor's exact mileage from the race station to the home left.

The birds are basketed the day before and put on a specially built chassis on the back of a truck and driven to the race station and released early in the morning. Each bird is wearing a counter mark or an electric band, which works like a bar code scanner at the supermarket. This records the time the pigeon arrives back home. Each loft is allowed to race as many 25 pigeons in a race.

The winner is determined by yards per minute. For example if I was competing against a bird from Orchard Park, my bird might have to fly an extra 20 miles to get home. Naturally the bird from Orchard Park would arrive sooner than my bird. If the birds were making 60 miles an hour, that would be a mile a minute. That means I would have to get a pigeon home in less than 20 minutes to beat him.

I've won our Memorial Race, which is the Buffalo club's biggest race young bird race, four times. Nobody else has won it that many times.

As important as they were to me, I'd trade all of those Memorial wins for just one Super Bowl ring.win.

Ed Abramoski's speech presenting Billy Shaw for induction to the Pro Football Hall of Fame in Canton Ohio, August 7, 1999.

Ladies and gentlemen, it is indeed a great honor to present to you Billy Shaw for induction into the National Football League Hall of Fame. Billy Shaw is the first player to be inducted into the Hall of Fame who played his entire career in the American Football League.

When the AFL was first formed, it was intended to be a league with teams that ran wide-open passing games. This was meant to be attractive to the fans. The Buffalo Bills deviated from this concept and indeed featured a grind-them-out running game, in which traps, off-tackle plays and end runs were the bread and butter of the offense. The success of this approach was mainly due to the ability of a good offensive line anchored by offensive guard Billy Shaw.

On account of the system used by most teams in the league, which was to pass first and run second, there were an awful lot of 40-30 games. For a time, the AFL was even nicknamed "a basketball league in cleats." This made for a very exciting game, appealing to the new AFL fans that had been eager for football in their hometowns. And for greater excitement, the league even made the football easier to pass by altering its shape. However, as I stated before, the Bills, who were very successful during those times, deviated from this approach by running the ball and running it well. Billy's playing ability was a large factor in the Bills' success.

Now, let me tell you some things about Billy. He was big. He was fast. He was intelligent, tenacious. As a matter of fact, Billy embodied all the words commonly used by coaches to describe the really great players.

Above all, Billy was extremely durable and dedicated. He was a trainer's dream, as many of the Bills players were. Through his career, he missed only part of the 1967 season due to a severe knee injury. Even then, Billy made it back onto the field much sooner than our medical staff had anticipated.

In those days, following knee surgery, it was common practice to put players in a cast for six weeks or so. When we removed Billy's cast, his knee had only 15 degrees of motion. He asked the doctor how soon he would be able to start lifting weights to build up the muscles around the knee. The doctor told him that as soon as he had full range of motion back the exercise program could begin.

Billy came back to me the next day with good range of motion. He asked me, "Abe, when do we start the weights?"

Befuddled, I asked him, "Billy, how did you accomplish this overnight?"

He told me he had put his young daughter on his ankle and lifted her up and down like a seesaw until he had his motion back. This clearly illustrates the type of drive and dedication Bill had then and has now.

During Billy's tenure with the team there was an on-going debate in the locker room as to whether Billy was truly fast or if the Bills' backs were really slow. Of course, the answer to that question depended on whom you asked. The linemen? Or the backs?

It was a pleasure to watch Billy pull out, kick out the linebacker, turn up field, get a piece of the cornerback and match, stride-for-stride, the running back as they ran down the field for a big gain or touchdown.

One day, during the normal banter in the training room I asked Billy what went through his mind as he pulled out to lead the play. In a fashion that was typically Billy, he told me that when he pulled out, he looked the linebacker in the face and if that linebacker looked really mean and had some teeth missing, he turned up field to block the little, 170-pound cornerback and left the mean, 215-pound linebacker for the fullback to deal with.

The old adage, behind every great man there is a great woman, certainly holds true for Billy Shaw. In his case, however, behind him stands his wife, Patsy, as well as his three daughters, Cindy, Cathy and Cheryl. Undoubtedly, without their years of love and support, Billy would not be here today. I offer my sincere congratulations to them and the rest of the Shaw family.

Mr. Ralph Wilson, the Buffalo Bills, Billy's former teammates and I and the fans in the City of Buffalo, who, incidentally, are here in great numbers, are extremely proud of Billy's upcoming induction into such a prestigious group. When one stops to consider the vast number of great players out there, whether just beginning in high school, continuing in college, playing in the NFL and all those that have played in the past, to be chosen as one of the elite is an honor beyond compare.

Ladies and gentlemen, may I present to you Mr. Billy Shaw. Thank you.

ABE'S AWARDS

1966   *Buffalo Bills Booster Club Inc.*
Special award for keeping players fit.

1974   *BAC- Broken Bone Award*
Buffalo Athletic Club

1986   *National Athletic Trainers Association Hall of Fame*
Display at Pro Football Hall of Fame, Canton, OH

1993   *Achievement in Field of Sports*
General K. Pulaski Assoc. Niagara Frontier

1996   *Greater Buffalo Sports Hall of Fame*
Display at HSBC Arena

1999   *Ralph Wilson Stadium – Wall of Fame*

1999   *New York State Athletic Trainers Assoc. Hall of Fame*
Display at Alumni Arena, University at Buffalo

ABE'S COMMENTS

on Famous Players and Coaches

Joe DeLamielleure:

"I remember coach (Lou) Saban telling him, 'It's heck to go to work every day and hate it.'...That was the first coach who ever told him don't give 110 percent to football in the off season... He and Billy Shaw are probably two best guards that ever played for the Bills."

Elbert Dubenion:

"Fastest thing ever.... Wilmer Fowler from Northwestern was on our team. He was the Big 10 dash co-champion.....and Duby could run right with those guys.

"I asked Duby, 'How fast can you run?' He said, 'Whatever it takes so the guys don't get me.'"

"He ran as fast as he had to. Nobody could run like him. That's why they called him 'Golden Wheels.'"

Joe Ferguson:

"He ranks right up there with the all-time best. Had he played with a team that had a real good defense or some good receivers, he would have been a fantastic football player. Very durable, very smart. Joe was his own worst enemy, in my opinion. He was a perfectionist. If he missed a pass or something happened, he always blamed himself and not the receiver for running the wrong route. If he got an interception in the first quarter and then completed 15 balls, he was still worrying about that interception."

Jack Kemp:

"I knew he'd be in politics. He used to spring his stuff on me and hear me out for a sounding board because I grew up in a Democratic neighborhood in Erie, Pa., where we were all steelworkers and factory workers.

"I knew he was destined. Nobody worked harder, no one tried harder. He was a good player, hard worker, had a fantastic arm, but a little erratic. A good football player. Not a great one, but way above average.

"I will vote for him… Whatever he does, he puts his heart and soul into it. He'll be really convinced that that will help the country. He won't do what's best for him, I really think he'll do what's best for the country."

Lou Saban:

"His philosophy was to get the offensive and defensive coordinator that wanted your job and control them…He asked me to go with him to Denver when he left. But I was very happy here. I fell in love with Buffalo."

Tom Sestak:

"Sestak to me was the best defensive player, with due respect to Bruce Smith. But he was in the same category with Bruce Smith. I think he belongs in the Pro Football Hall of Fame. Sestak was a fantastic football player. He had bad knees and never practiced his last two years and still made All-Pro."

Billy Shaw:

"Bill was the first big lineman who could really run. And when he would go out in front of that ball-carrier, he was something else.

"We asked him, 'When you pull around that end and you see that guy, what do you think of?'

"He said 'When I look at him, if he looks at me and he's smiling and he has all his teeth in and he has no scars on him, I go right into him full tilt. But if he looks like he's got four teeth missing, I block him very gingerly."

O.J. Simpson:

"The finest runner I've ever seen play. He was a big guy that never really took a big hit. He never really got tackled hard. He knew when to give in and when to go down....One time he got hurt in the corner of the end zone and I got hurt going out to help him. I didn't know what to do. I pulled my calf muscle and I thought somebody shot me from the stand. I didn't know whether to sit down or fall down, so we walked off the field and people thought I was showing O.J. how to walk off the field with an injury."

Ralph Wilson:

"I still don't think he has the respect that's really due him from a lot of people in town. I remember when we first came, they said he was an out-of-towner and stuff like that and didn't have the city at heart.

"But I really think he does. I think the people have realized in the last five or 10 years that he wants to win and he's really a good person."

Here I am pre-game with my longtime friend and boss.

OUT OF THE MOUTH OF ABE....

Here are some of Abe's "famous" wisecracks and comeback lines:

I've seen better legs on a pool table.

You've got a heart like a blowtorch.

Your mouth goes like a whip-o-will's butt during mating season.

Who? Who? You're no owl. Your feet don't fit no limb.

I get paid weekly. Very weakly.

It's raining like a cow pissing on a flat rock.

He went by him like a pay car past a bum.

Shut your butt and give your face a chance.

You have a headache. You probably have the gout and need to stand on the slant board.

If we have a battle of wits, you've got half a chance.

If bullshit were electricity, you'd be a powerhouse.

Styles comes and goes, class lasts.

You still have your first communion money.

If you had a brain cell, your entire family would fight for it.

If your brain were made of gasoline, you wouldn't have enough gas to power a piss-ant on a motorcycle halfway around a BB.

You should sue your legs for non-support. Your calves are like a cowboy, you're always having a roundup.

He couldn't coach his way out of a wet paper bag.

Frank, Diet Coke would pay you not to be seen drinking their drink.

How about lending me a half a hundred until my hunchbacked brother straightens out.

You can speed up Mother Nature, but you can't get ahead of her.

Find the cause; don't treat the symptom.

You've got to get better to die.

Of all the athletes I have known, you are one of them.

He's got a heart like a pea.

You came in second place — everyone else tied for first.

I'll have a large pizza with everything on it and a diet coke.

Stick with me and I'll have you farting through silk.

You are the best I know, Baby. (Ken Johnson)

Tony Marchitte made Abe what he is today. Too bad Tony is not here to explain it to us. (Bud Tice)

If you have a cold and we medicate you for it, it will take a week to get over it. If we leave it alone, it will take seven days.

We are treating him with scientific neglect.

I've got pigeons with a bigger heart than that guy has.

It's a dirty, four-letter word — W-O-R-K.

I've known people to get over polio faster than you're getting over that sprained ankle.

I've got mine. (Marchitte when you ask him for raingear during a game on the road.)

I'm OK, Abe, but how are the fans taking it (Old Tom "Tippy" Day line).

Your definition of humility is true self-esteem.

I don't know what they're paying Charley McCarthy for, as funny as you are.

There are two things keeping me from springing on you – fear and common sense.

Anybody taking you for an asshole knows what they're talking about.

He's so cheap, he squeezes a nickel so hard the Indian comes out riding a buffalo.

It's better to wear out than to rust out.

Sitting still and wishing makes no person great. The Good Lord sends the fish in, but you must dig the bait.

You're so smart, your next six thoughts will be your first half-dozen.

EPILOGUE

Birth of a New Bills Era

There's never a dull moment in football and especially with the Buffalo Bills. As the final touches and editing were being put on this book an exciting new chapter in Bills' history is about to begin.

That of course is the arrival of quarterback Drew Bledsoe and the other new Bills such as first-round draft choice Mike Williams, the offensive tackle from Texas and linebackers London Fletcher and Eddie Robinson, who were signed as free agents. Besides Williams, who is built along the same lines as Howard Ballard, one of the tackles on our Super Bowl teams, the Bills added an experienced offensive lineman in Trey Teague from Denver.

Those are significant additions.

Earlier, in the book I told of how the arrival of Jim Kelly in 1986 signaled the start of a new day for the Bills. I felt confident he could lead us to winning ways.

Call it déjà vu or whatever you want, but I got the same feeling with the news of the Bledsoe trade.

There are a lot of parallels between now and 1986. Back then we were coming off two straight 2-14 seasons and we seemed to have lost confidence in our ability to ever win again. The morale of the fans was down too. You could tell that by the attendance and that carried over to the players on the field, to the coaches and even down to the trainers' room. You can always do your job better when you are hopeful and upbeat.

Now along comes Bledsoe. After all the success of the 1990s, the Bills and the fans suffered through a dismal 2001 season, 3-13. I knew things would eventually get better with the draft and free agency, but I thought it would take time unless something big happened.

In 1986 that something big was Jim Kelly. In 2002, that something big could be Drew Bledsoe. He's a proven pro, who I think will make our other players better. I can see big things for a player like Eric Moulds with Bledsoe throwing to him. Having an experience pro with a strong arm should make everybody more confident - the offensive line, running backs and receivers. And it should carry over to the defense, too.

Like all fans, I'm looking forward to this new era of Bills football with the new football uniforms and a new attitude.

I'm no Mr. Blackwell, but I like the look of the new uniforms. I especially like the return of the blue pants to go with the white road jerseys.

You could tell that a new feeling of optimism carried over to the fans just by the size of the turnout for the unveiling of the new uniforms and the reception Bledsoe received at the stadium when he first came to town.

I think it will be as much fun as the previous 42 years, most of which I was fortunate to be a part of.

Here I am celebrating with 2002 Pro Football Hall of Famer Jim Kelly.

ABOUT THE AUTHORS

Eddie "Abe" Abramoski

From Cookie Gilchrist to Jim Kelly, Steve Tasker to Mack Yoho, Hall of Fame trainer Eddie "Abe" Abramoski was at the heart of the Buffalo Bills every day as the team trainer. When an injury during his college days at Purdue ended his playing career, "Abe" turned to training, learning the profession under the great Pinky Newell. Five years later, he landed in Buffalo as the first trainer of the new Buffalo Bills and stayed on the job for 37 years, through thick and thin, through championship seasons in the old American Football League, through four Super Bowl years in the 1990s.

During that time, he became one of the most identifiable of Bills to outsiders. Every player and coach who passed through Buffalo over the years remembers "Abe." He was more than a trainer. He was also a friend, confidant of many. A walking history book on the Bills. In this book, he shares some of the humorous - and some touching - stories and memories of his long tenure with the team.

Abramoski is on the Bills' Wall of Fame at Ralph Wilson Stadium. He is also a member of the Greater Buffalo Sports Hall of Fame and the National Trainers Association Hall of Fame. Ed and his wife,Pat, are the parents of five daughters and have 13 grandchildren.

Now retired, "Abe" lives in Amherst, N.Y., where he spends his spare time at his long-time hobby, pigeon racing.

Milt Northrop

Since he arrived in Buffalo in 1967, Milt Northrop covered virtually every conceivable sport for the Buffalo News. From 1981 to 1990, he was the paper's lead reporter on the Bills. Prior to that he covered the Buffalo Braves of the NBA for eight years. Sabres, Bisons and even the Royals, Stampede and Wings, he covered them all, too, as well as a variety of college sports and was a correspondent to The Sporting News, Sports Illustrated and Basketball Weekly.

Before that he covered college high school and professional sports for newspapers in his native Connecticut.

The 1959 graduate of the University of Connecticut is a sports historian with particular interest in college football and basketball as well as the NFL.

He lives in Williamsville, N.Y. with his wife, Michele. They are the parents of five children.

Milt Northrop (standing) and Ed Abramoski
have known each other for more than 30 years.